LIBERTARIAN
ANARCHY

THINK NOW

Think Now is a new series of books which examines central contemporary social and political issues from a philosophical perspective. These books aim to be accessible, rather than overly technical, bringing philosophical rigour to modern questions which matter the most to us. Provocative yet engaging, the authors take a stand on political and cultural themes of interest to any intelligent reader.

AVAILABLE NOW:

Beyond Animal Rights, Tony Milligan

Ethics of Climate Change, James Garvey

Ethics of Metropolitan Growth, Robert Kirkman

Ethics of Trade and Aid, Christopher D. Wraight

Historical Redress, Richard Vernon

Just Warriors Inc., Deane-Peter Baker

Nanoethics, Donal P. O'Mathuna

Personal Responsibility, Alexander Brown

Terrorism, Nicholas Fotion

War and Ethics, Nicholas Fotion

SERIES EDITORS:

James Garvey is Secretary of the Royal Institute of Philosophy, UK. He is the author of *The Twenty Greatest Philosophy Books* and *The Ethics of Climate Change*, also published by Continuum.

Jeremy Stangroom is co-editor, with Julian Baggini, of *The Philosophers' Magazine* and co-author of *Why Truth Matters*, *What Philosophers Think* and *Great Thinkers A-Z* (all Continuum).

LIBERTARIAN ANARCHY

ANARCHY

Against the state

GERARD CASEY

continuum

Continuum International Publishing Group

| 50 Bedford Square | 80 Maiden Lane |
| London WC1B 3DP | New York NY 10038 |

www.continuumbooks.com

© Gerard Casey, 2012

First published 2012
Reprinted 2012

British Library Cataloguing-in-Publication Data
A catalogue record for this book is available from the British Library.

ISBN: HB: 978-1-4411-2552-1
PB: 978-1-4411-4467-6

Library of Congress Cataloging-in-Publication Data
Casey, Gerard, 1951-
Libertarian anarchy : against the state / Gerard Casey.
pages cm. – (Think now)
Includes bibliographical references and index.
ISBN 978-1-4411-4467-6 (pbk. : alk. paper) – ISBN 978-1-4411-2552-1
(hardcover : alk. paper) – ISBN 978-1-4411-0338-3 (ebook epub : alk. paper) –
ISBN 978-1-4411-4961-9 (ebook pdf : alk. paper)
1. Anarchism–Philosophy. 2. State, The–Philosophy. I. Title.

HX833.C37 2012
335'.83–dc23

2011048717

Typeset by Newgen Imaging Systems Pvt Ltd, Chennai, India
Printed and bound in the United States

CONTENTS

7 Conclusion 146

ACKNOWLEDGEMENTS

I have to thank my long-suffering colleagues in University College Dublin for listening to me rabbiting on about libertarianism and anarchism *ad nauseam* and for being far too polite to tell me I'm talking through my hat. I am particularly grateful to my academic next-door neighbour Brian O'Connor for strolling into my room from time to time and asking questions beginning with, 'What would libertarians say about . . .?' The support of my former mentor in philosophy, Garrett Barden, is much appreciated. His conversation is always delightfully lucid, precise, elegant and insightful. Thanks are due to my students, postgraduate and undergraduate, who made (and make) the teaching of this material to them a positive pleasure. They have been in turn bewildered, incredulous, outraged, enthusiastic, but always argumentative and engaged.

I am very grateful to the Ludwig von Mises Institute for regularly allowing me to present my ideas at the annual Austrian Scholars Conference (ASC) convened by Dr Joseph Salerno. In a world where academic conferences routinely resemble a set of intellectual penitential exercises the ASC provides unmatched intellectual stimulation while also being possibly the only place on earth where I can be made to feel insufficiently radical.

I have been thinking about these matters for some years now and some of my thoughts have been published in different forms in various outlets. I have reused some of this material, integrating it into the larger narrative, and I am grateful to the publications involved for permission to republish. Particulars are noted where appropriate.

I make no claims to novelty for anything I have said but console myself with the thought expressed by one of my heroes, St Thomas More, that an absolutely new idea is one of the rarest things known to man. Rather than strive for novelty, I have attempted, perhaps unfashionably, to say what I think is true. I could, of course, be wrong since attempt, alas, isn't necessarily the same thing as achievement.

Everything that I have read in preparation for writing this book (at least in the last year or so) is listed in the Bibliography and I cannot sufficiently express my gratitude to those who wrote this material, both those whom I consider to have illuminated the issues in ways I find congenial and those whom I consider to have proposed really tough and interesting alternatives to my position. If I have misquoted anyone or, even worse, failed to credit someone's words or ideas, I apologise and will do my best to rectify matters as and when appropriate.

I very much appreciate the help of Patricia Casey, Jason Walsh and Peter White in reading and commenting on the manuscript. Apart from picking up numerous typographical errors, they also forced me to make this book something written in a language that has some connection with idiomatic English rather than being expressed in that strange and incomprehensible academic dialect I have learnt over too many years in what some wit once called 'the graves of academe'.

1
INTRODUCTION

The criminal state

States are criminal organizations. All states, not just the obviously totalitarian or repressive ones. The only possible exceptions to this sweeping claim are those mini-states that are, in effect, swollen bits of private property, such as the Vatican. I intend this statement to be understood literally and not as some form of rhetorical exaggeration. The argument is simple. Theft, robbery, kidnapping and murder are all crimes. Those who engage in such activities, whether on their own behalf or on behalf of others are, by definition, criminals. In taxing the people of a country, the state engages in an activity that is morally equivalent to theft or robbery; in putting some people in prison, especially those who are convicted of so-called victimless crimes or when it drafts people into the armed services, the state is guilty of kidnapping or false imprisonment; in engaging in wars that are other than purely defensive or, even if defensive, when the means of defence employed are disproportionate and indiscriminate, the state is guilty of manslaughter or murder.

For many people, perhaps most, these contentions will seem both shocking and absurd. Some will immediately object that taxation is clearly not theft. They may say as Craig Duncan does[1] that since you do not have legal title to all your pre-tax income the state commits no crime in appropriating that part of your income to which it is entitled. The problem with this objection is that it completely begs the question – *is* the state entitled to part of your income?

The libertarian contention that taxation is the moral equivalent of theft can be true, Duncan believes, only if people have a moral right 'to keep and control all their earnings'[2] but this claim, he thinks, is beset with fatal problems. To illustrate this point, he rehearses the tragedy of Annie the antiques dealer who has to hand over 20 per cent of her earnings to the owner of the premises she rents to conduct her business. If Annie were to claim that she had a right to all her earnings and should not be obliged to fork over the 20 per cent, the building owner will respond that without his premises, she would not have been able to make any sales in the first place. 'Something similar', says Duncan, 'is true of government taxes'.[3] If it were not for the state's enforcing contracts, protecting property rights, keeping the peace, printing currency, preventing monopolies and so on, you or anyone else would not be able to go about your daily business. So, the argument goes, by analogy the state has a moral entitlement to a portion of your earnings, at least to an amount sufficient to cover the costs of the services the state provides.

This analogy is so weak it not only limps, as most analogies do, but it positively staggers around on one leg. First of all, Annie presumably has made an agreement with her landlord and did so freely. If she does not want to hand over 20 per cent of her earnings to him, she can try to renegotiate the contract or take her business elsewhere. In stark contrast, the average citizen has made no agreement with the state. The state unilaterally determines the amount that citizens must 'pay'. Citizens are not at liberty to take their 'business' elsewhere since the state forcibly excludes competitors who might be willing to supply more cheaply the services provided by the state. Duncan's analogy, if it has any force at all, has it only if it runs in the opposite direction. On the libertarian way of thinking about it, taking commercial relations as the norm, Annie Citizen is forced to do her business in premises of her landlord's (the state's) choosing, paying whatever rent he (the state) determines he deserves, and her landlord (the state) can legitimately use violence to prevent someone else offering her a better deal.

Some will reject the charge of false imprisonment or kidnapping that I lay against the state. People are put in gaol, they will say, only if they are convicted of committing a crime; the fact that they are in gaol means they are criminals. The state is not only not doing anything wrong in putting them there, it is doing something positively good by protecting us from these miscreants. This objection, of course, draws our attention firmly to the question of which courses of conduct actually constitute crime. While most people will agree that murder, robbery, kidnapping and assault are crimes involving, as they do, gross interference with the lives, liberties and properties of others, it is not entirely clear just what awful deed is being done by Tom, Dick and Harriet when, for example, they smoke pot in the privacy of their rooms and why it should require violent intervention by the state to prevent it.

Through taxation, the state aggresses against the property of the individual and, through the variety of compulsory monopolies it enjoys, the state aggresses against the free exchange of goods and services in the area of which it claims control. Murray Rothbard writes that 'the State, which subsists on taxation, is a vast criminal organization, far more formidable and successful than any "private" Mafia in history'. He makes the point that 'it should be considered criminal' not according to some idiosyncratic conception of criminality but 'according to the common apprehension of mankind, which always considers theft to be a crime'.[4] As the satirist, H. L. Mencken, notes, 'The intelligent man, when he pays taxes, certainly does not believe that he is making a prudent and productive investment of his money; on the contrary, he feels that he is being mulcted in an excessive amount for services that, in the main, are useless to him, and that, in substantial part, are downright inimical to him.'[5]

Unless you work for the state, your direct encounters with it are likely to be unpleasant. Think of being manhandled at an airport and made to feel as if you were a criminal but not wanting to protest in case the securicrats deem you a security threat and detain you. If you have ever had to deal with the state's bureaucrats in, let us say, an immigration department, you will have firsthand experience of what Shakespeare calls 'the insolence of office'. Perhaps you are one of the thousands of people who have been pulled over by a man in uniform for 'speeding' in an area where the speed limit is set arbitrarily low, when it is patently obvious that the function of the speeding ticket is not, in fact, to promote road safety but simply to raise revenue? If you are an employer, are you happy that you are obliged to act as an involuntary unpaid tax collector, removing large chunks of your employees' wages for remittance to the Tax Office while also being forced to bear the costs in time and money of this collection and remittance?

What makes these encounters unpleasant in a way that your dealings with commercial bodies are normally not unpleasant is that, as Jan Narveson puts it, 'agents of government have a relation to you that nobody else normally has'. If you get poor service in a restaurant, you can protest. If your mobile phone refuses to function, you can take it back to the store and demand an exchange or get your money back. But if you do not like what you are made to go through at an airport do not even think of protesting; and if you think you pay too much in tax, just what do you propose to do about it? 'Government', as Narveson says, 'can "do bad things to you" and they can make it stick. . . . The law, literally, is on their side: They claim, indeed, to *be* "the law." If you disagree – well, too bad for you!'[6]

Societies governed by states are divided into those who rule and those who are ruled.[7] Rulers associate in a mutually beneficial symbiotic relationship with those who can be useful to them, granting them privileges such as monopolies or quasi-monopolies or allowing them to operate in ways not available to the mass of individuals or genuinely private businesses. For example, because of state guarantees to underwrite banking defaults and because deposits are treated legally as loans, banks – all banks – are allowed to operate in bankrupt mode. This privilege – literally, this private law – is not accorded to ordinary businesses. Much of what is described as capitalism is actually a contemporary form of mercantilism in which certain economic actors, usually powerful and wealthy ones, seek and obtain privileges from the state in return for their support. Capitalism (mercantilism) of this sort is simply an extension of the state's activities and so, from a libertarian perspective, is indefensible.[8] Not only is it indefensible it is also wildly incompetent, as witnessed by the current, sustained (2008–12) global financial crisis induced primarily by the actions and policies of states, state agencies and their friends who operate businesses (especially banks) that are considered too big to fail.

Libertarianism and anarchism – an overview

Anarchy is the position in which the members of a society naturally finds themselves when they are not subject to the power of a state. The theory that argues for the desirability of such a condition is *anarchism*.[9] Anarchism comes in two varieties: philosophical and practical. Philosophical anarchists argue for the illegitimacy of the state regardless of whether or not any of the alternatives to it are productive of better outcomes for individuals apart, of course, from the enhancement of liberty. Practical anarchists, on the other hand, argue that anarchy is feasible, that its outcomes would be better as a whole for all (though not, of course, for state dependants) and that efforts should be made to bring it about. Of course, there is nothing to stop someone being both a philosophical anarchist and a practical anarchist; nonetheless, in this book, I shall present the argument for anarchism primarily in its philosophical variety.[10]

The standard political options in modern democracies are liberalism and conservatism. Though they differ from each other in many respects, both are content to use the power of the state to promote their policies. Liberals are content to use the power of the state to enforce their economic views on all in respect of what they consider to be the appropriate distribution of goods and services while they claim as large a liberty as possible for personal, especially sexual, morality.

Conservatives, on the other hand, generally wish to have as much liberty as possible for economic activities while recruiting the power of the state to enforce their moral views on others. Libertarians differ from both contemporary liberals and conservatives in that they reject the use of force in all cases except where it is necessary to resist or punish aggression. For libertarians, liberty operates as a fundamental principle across the whole range of human endeavour in contrast to both liberals and conservatives who are selective about the areas in which liberty is allowed to hold sway.

It might be as well to clarify one popular misconception right at the start: libertarianism is *not* the same thing as libertinism. It is true that libertarianism will not admit the physical restraint or physical punishment of acts that do not aggress against others but it nowhere implies moral approval of such acts or rules out their restraint by other methods such as exhortation, boycotting or loudly expressed disapproval. Take, for example, the issues of pornography, prostitution, adultery and homosexuality. In dealing with issues such as these, the libertarian invokes the distinction between the immoral and the illegal. The crux of the matter is not whether pornography, for example, is immoral or degrading or whether it is a uninhibited expression of spontaneous sexuality. Such matters are relevant to determining the morality of pornography; they are irrelevant to the question of whether or not pornography should be legally prohibited. The only question here, for the libertarian, is whether the law should be used to enforce a particular morality where the issue in question does not pertain to the matter of defending people against aggression directed at their persons or property. The libertarian answer is clear – the law has no business enforcing purely moral considerations. Libertarians may well find such activities morally reprehensible (or not) but they will argue that it is no part of the law to prohibit or regulate such activities unless they involve aggression.

Libertarians reject state control or regulation of the media for whatever purpose. From the libertarian point of view, publishers, reporters, writers, commentators and film directors are responsible for what they write, tell or show and individual readers and viewers are responsible for what they are prepared to read or to see. If you do not want to see something, do not look. If you do not want to hear something, do not listen. TVs and radios come with switches that turn them off as well as turning them on. If you feel really strongly about some issue or other, say a particular TV programme, you may organize a non-violent boycott of the show's advertisers or write a letter of protest to the station manager – you may use any non-violent method you choose to achieve your aim. But you may *not* initiate aggression and you may *not* recruit others, including the state, to act aggressively on your behalf.

While libertarians may be willing to concede that the use of many chemical substances is individually and socially harmful, they will oppose attempts to proscribe or regulate either drug-taking or drug commerce. This for two reasons. The first, principled, reason is that such proscription or regulation is a violation of individual liberty; the second, consequentialist, reason, is that history shows that such attempts at proscription and regulation inevitably make a bad situation worse. Alcohol prohibition of the 1920s was an unqualified disaster and today's so-called war on drugs is no more successful in reducing the incidence of drug-taking. (Isn't it remarkable that whereas in the good old days we used to wage war on countries, nations or states, now we wage war on inanimate objects like drugs and abstract nouns like terrorism?) The 'war on drugs' merely increases the price of drugs to consumers and profits to retailers, corrupts those charged with enforcing the anti-drug laws and ensures that large numbers of people who otherwise would not come to the attention of the police receive a first class criminal training at the public expense in state-run penal facilities. Legal and physical compulsion is not a sound foundation upon which to build the moral character of individuals or a better society.

What of compulsory school attendance? Libertarians reject it. State-enforced school attendance is a form of involuntary incarceration that violates the rights of both parents and children. Only the parents or guardians of children and the children when they are old enough to assume responsibility for themselves can make such decisions. What goes for compulsory school attendance goes even more for military conscription. Conscription is sometimes justified on the grounds that we need it to defend our countries. Unless we equate our countries with the states operating in our countries, and putting to one side the obvious point that if there are no states there would be no states to attack or be attacked, the libertarian will argue that conscription is a form of involuntary servitude – more bluntly, a form of slavery – and so is to be rejected on libertarian grounds.

Immigration? Libertarians, for the most part, will support immigration. There's nothing special about the territory of a particular state. If someone is willing to hire or sponsor an immigrant that should be the end of the matter. The availability of tax-supported social welfare for immigrants tends to skew arguments on this issue but then welfare, whether individual or corporate, is not something that your average libertarian is likely to be supportive of in any case. Bailouts for businesses? Libertarians reject them. No one is entitled to demand that others be forcibly required to support his business, whatever that business may be, whether farming, shoemaking or banking.

It should now be apparent how the libertarian is prepared to analyse a whole range of practical matters – trade tariffs, wage floors and wage ceilings, military interventions abroad, fiscal policy, gun control and nuclear power. When it comes to considering whether to recognize actions or behaviours as criminal, we must ask if they involve aggression against the person or properties of others. If not, whatever view one may entertain of their morality or desirability, they should not be the subject of legal prohibition.

Roadmap

This book has a limited number of objectives: to show the anti-libertarian character of states and state action, to argue for the presumption of liberty, to make the case for libertarian anarchy, to show that law does not require state sponsorship and to demonstrate the illegitimacy of the modern state by means of an attack on the representative nature of democracy and the validity of state constitutions.

In Chapter 2, I exhibit the criminal character of the state, illustrating this by looking at where the state comes from and showing what it does, particularly in the matter of war-making and tax-exaction. The state is said to be necessary for many things – the provision of roads, water, public services and so on – and while it can be and has been shown that none of these things requires a state to provide it, there is always one set of services that the defender of the state will retreat to when pressed, namely, that the state is necessary for the provision of justice, law and order. If I can show that justice, law and order can be provided without a state, then the state begins to look like the Wizard of Oz, a small man with a megaphone pulling levers behind a curtain. Chapter 3 outlines an account of liberty that is consistent with the moral character of human action without which human life is meaningless. In Chapter 4, I give an account of anarchy and conclude that the combination of liberty and anarchy is antecedently persuasive. Chapter 5 attempts to show, both theoretically and practically, that it is possible to have law without a state. I show how law originates spontaneously as a concomitant attribute of every society and has no necessary connection to a state. In Chapter 6, I undermine the most popular justifications for the modern democratic state – that in this form of the state we really rule ourselves and that constitutions provide a solution to the perennial problem of political consent.

Perhaps the deepest and most pervasive illusion of statists is that we can escape from anarchy and that the means of escape is the state. But can we? I hope to show (briefly) in what follows that in fact we always live in some condition of anarchy at some level or other and that the only decision we have to make is what kind of anarchy we want to live with. Will it be the political anarchy of competing state branches *within* states and the anarchy of competition *between* states on the international stage, or will it be the emergent order of libertarian anarchy that is the natural condition of human beings who take their freedoms (and their corresponding responsibilities) seriously?[11]

I am painfully aware that there are many issues of importance I will not have touched on in the book. You will probably find the phrase 'But what about . . .?' forming in your head from time to time as you read. I can only plead in extenuation that in a book of such modest proportions I have had to be extremely selective in my choice of topics. Others faced with a similar problem would, no doubt, have chosen to do things differently, keeping some things that I have eliminated and eliminating some things that I have kept, but *quod scripsi, scripsi*, what I have written, I have written.

2
DEATH AND TAXES

The state – necessary and legitimate?

Political theory and political practice are dominated by a myth, the myth of the *necessity* and the *legitimacy* of the state. While there can be genuine disagreement about what it is that the term 'state' properly applies to, for the purposes of this book I am going to take the state to be that group of people or that organization which wields a monopoly of allegedly legitimate force over the inhabitants of a determinate territory financed by a compulsory levy imposed on those inhabitants. This working definition of the state may not be universally acceptable but neither is it idiosyncratic. For example the eminent historian Charles Tilly in one place defines states as 'relatively centralized, differentiated organizations the officials of which more or less successfully claim control over the chief concentrated means of violence within a population inhabiting a large, contiguous territory'[1] and in another as 'coercion-wielding organizations that are distinct from households and kinship groups and exercise clear priority in some respects over all other organizations within substantial territories'.[2] Robert Ellickson describes that state as 'a hierarchical organization that is widely regarded as having the legitimate authority to inflict detriments on persons (within its geographically defined jurisdiction) who have not necessarily voluntarily submitted themselves to its authority'.[3] While not absolutely identical to each other, these definitions come to pretty much the same thing in the end and are essentially the same as mine. They all hark back to Max Weber's classic statement that 'a state is a human community that (successfully) claims the *monopoly of the legitimate use of physical force* within a given territory'.[4] Significantly, a little before presenting his now classic definition, Weber wrote: 'If no social institutions existed which knew the use of violence, then the concept of "state" would be eliminated, and a condition would emerge that could be designated as "anarchy," in the specific sense of this word. . . . force is a means specific to the state.'[5] Murray Rothbard's definition of the State follows the Weberean pattern in characterizing the state as an organization that achieves a compulsory monopoly of force and ultimate decision-making power over a given territorial area but adds an element not explicitly present in it, namely, that the state 'acquires its revenue by physical coercion'.[6]

For some writers, state and government effectively amount to pretty much the same thing; others distinguish between them. For those who do so distinguish, government is generally presented in concrete terms as a group of individuals acting in a certain capacity while the state is presented abstractly as the more or less permanent organization that functions independently of any particular set of individuals. So, for example Crispin Sartwell defines a government as a group of people who in fact exercise coercive control (control backed by violence or the threat of violence) over others in a given area.[7] In contrast, he thinks of the state as an abstract entity, as a way of conceptualizing a government as a kind of corporation that can exist and continue to exist even when the personnel of the government change. For most practical purposes, it makes little difference whether we refer to states or governments. Throughout this book I will use the term 'state' for preference, not least because, on the anarchic conception of society I present and defend below, some voluntary modes of social organization can have governing structures (and hence governments) while not being states.

The state is considered *necessary* for the provision of many things but primarily for the provision of peace and security by means of its powers of law-making, law adjudication and law enforcement. The dominant myth holds that without the state there would be widespread disorder, violence and chaos in society; in a word, anarchy. Without the state and its laws, we would live in a world 'where everyone is free to grab anything he can without ever being obliged to justify his conduct before any institution charged with settling disputes'.[8] The rejection of this claim is one of the central themes of this book. The state is considered *legitimate* inasmuch as the force it employs or threatens to employ in pursuit of its goals is considered to be justified ultimately by the consent of those to whom it is applied. The rejection of the state's claim to legitimacy is another central theme of this book.

In describing the idea that the state is necessary and legitimate as a myth, I am not merely saying euphemistically that it is an idea that happens not to be true. For me, myths are foundational narratives, the ultimate framing devices in the context of which our humdrum day-to-day beliefs and practices find their place. Such myths, whatever their ultimate truth, have the peculiar property that they cannot be called into question from within – from that point of view, their falsity is literally unthinkable. The English philosopher, R. G. Collingwood[9] referred to such a set of myths as 'absolute presuppositions'; similarly, Wittgenstein[10] recognized a functional class of propositions as 'standing fast' in relation to any given mode of thought. Because we see through myths, that is *by means of* them, we find it difficult to see through them, that is to recognize their lack of foundation and their radical contingency.

The belief in the legitimacy and necessity of the state is a prime example of a myth. So dominant is it that the position this book proposes – that the state as we know it today is historically contingent, functionally unnecessary and illegitimate – is typically met with a mixture of bewilderment, incredulity, derision and hostility. For many, if not most, people such a claim is either practically inconceivable or unimaginable. A moment's reflection will suffice to displace this prejudice. Cast your mind back to the beginnings of human history and you will immediately see that, as James Scott remarks 'Until shortly before the common era, the very last 1 per cent of human history, the social landscape consisted of elementary, self-governing, kinship units that might, occasionally, cooperate in hunting, feasting, skirmishing, trading and peacemaking' but, he continues significantly, 'It did not contain anything one could call a state. In other words, living in the absence of state structures has been the standard human condition.'[11] My aim in this book is to make the historical contingency, functional lack of necessity and illegitimacy of the state both conceivable and imaginable.

The origin and character of the state

Any discussion of how the state originated has to speculate about what happened in human prehistory. Because human prehistory is *pre*history we do not have records available to us from which we can construct our narrative so our conclusions are necessarily conjectural. This form of speculation has a venerable ancestry and early examples can be found in Immanuel Kant's *Conjectural Beginnings of Human History*[12] and Adam Smith's *Lectures in Jurisprudence*. In the latter, Smith writes that 'There are four distinct states which mankind pass thro': – 1st, the Age of Hunters; 2ndly, the Age of Shepherds; 3rdly, the Age of Agriculture; and 4thly, the Age of Commerce.'[13] It is very likely that the first really significant shift in human culture took place when mankind discovered agriculture, in Smith's typology, when human beings moved from stage two to stage three.[14] Instead of chasing after their moveable food source and collecting what non-moveable food items lay about until either or both were exhausted, some group of early humans had the bright idea of domesticating both animals and plants so guaranteeing for themselves, natural disasters apart, a reliable supply of food. This revolution in human culture provided for those human beings who adopted it a relatively more secure source of food than did hunting and gathering or simple pastoralism and, crucially, permitted them to settle permanently in one place. The increased productivity resulting from this first agricultural revolution made possible a more sophisticated division of labour than that which allocated hunting tasks to men and gathering tasks to women. For the first time in human history, a significant number of people were released from the time-consuming burden of earning their livings by the sweat of their brows and could turn their attention to other things – some good, some not so good.

You can make a living in two ways: the first way is to produce and exchange goods and services; the second way is to allow others to produce and exchange and to take the fruits of their labours from them by force.[15] Franz Oppenheimer famously remarked, 'There are two fundamentally opposed means whereby man, requiring sustenance, is impelled to obtain the necessary means for satisfying his desires. These are work and robbery, one's own labor and the forcible appropriation of the labor of others.' He termed one's own labour and the exchange of that labour for another's labour the *economic means* for the satisfaction of needs while the unilateral appropriation of another's labour he termed the *political means*.[16] For some people, theft or robbery is always more attractive than solid toil and if human nature has not changed fundamentally over the last 50,000 years, it is safe to assume that even in pre-agricultural societies, human predation upon human was a reasonably popular option, at least outside one's immediate kinship group. As Thomas Hobbes notes, 'And in all places, where men have lived by small Families, to robbe and spoyle one another, has been a Trade, and so farre from being reputed against the Law of nature, that the greater spoyles they gained, the greater was their honour. . . .'[17] However, given the small-scale, transient character and low productivity of pre-agricultural societies the prospects for long-term large-scale predation was severely limited. With the coming of the agricultural revolution, all that changed forever.[18]

Just as agriculture involves the shift from hunting animals to domesticating them, so too the political means, the method of the incipient state, originates in the move from simply robbing and killing other people more or less indiscriminately to, as it were, domesticating them and taking a portion of their produce from them at regular intervals instead of taking everything they possess in one fell swoop. We might see this as the *agriculturalization of predation* (what Mancur Olson calls stationary banditry[19]) which, as a long-term strategy, is much more productive than outright confiscation and destruction. For a latter-day (fictional) example of this, think of the film *The Magnificent Seven* in which the villagers who live in the valley grow the crops that the bandits who live in the hills take from them by force, leaving them enough to live on so that they may continue to produce and be robbed again and again. Oppenheimer argues that the state is ultimately dependent and parasitic upon the economic means generated by society: 'No state, therefore, can come into being until the economic means has created a definite number of objects for the satisfaction of needs, which objects may be taken away or appropriated by warlike robbery.'[20]

One finds an astonishing degree of agreement among scholars that the state and violence are intimately related. If you were to ask David Hume how the state originated he would say that 'Almost all the governments which exist at present, or of which there remains any record in story, have been founded originally in usurpation or conquest or both, without any pretense of a fair consent or voluntary subjection of the people.'[21] Charles Tilly, too, is not guilty of reticence on this matter, for the very title of his seminal 1985 article is 'War Making and State Making as Organized Crime.' Anthony de Jasay writes that, as a matter of fact, the real life states that people actually endure have come into existence because their ancestors 'were beaten into obedience by an invader, and sometimes due to Hobson's choice' had to take one king so as to escape the threat of getting another[22] while Crispin Sartwell remarks that 'Almost any realistic view of the origin of states will attribute their founding or at any rate their development and preservation, to the large-scale application of violence.'[23] The renowned attorney Clarence S. Darrow rejects as a fairy story for children the idea that states came into existence to discourage and punish the evil and the lawless and to protect the weak and helpless.

On the contrary, he claims, history shows that 'the state was born in aggression, and that in all the various stages through which it has passed its essential characteristics have been preserved'.[24] The action of the state 'rests on violence and force; is sustained by soldiers, policemen, and courts; and is contrary to the ideal peace and order that make for the happiness and progress of the human race'.[25]

Although the emergence of what Oppenheimer terms the political means and the economic means must coincide in large part with the increase in productivity made possible by the agricultural revolution, our historical knowledge of precisely what happened and when is necessarily speculative. Our earliest records show the presence of modes of social organization that could be regarded as states of some sort dating back almost ten thousand years in the area known as the Fertile Crescent.[26] These early states took the form of cities surrounded and supported by a productive tribute-paying hinterland. Some thousands of years later we witness the emergence from these city-states of the first empires subsisting on tribute exacted by force from conquered neighbours. James Scott notes that 'much, if not most, of the population of the early states was unfree; they were subjects under duress'. To live in such a state rendered one liable for 'taxes, conscription, corvée labor' and implied for most of its inhabitants a 'condition of servitude'. In substance, then, these early states were 'warmaking machines . . . producing hemorrhages of subjects fleeing conscription, invasion and plunder'.[27]

States of one kind or another may have been around for some ten thousand years or so but the state in its modern and contemporary form is of relatively recent vintage. Harold Berman, in his now classic *Law and Revolution*, argues for the emergence of the West from events that happened in the eleventh century.[28] Tilly, too, sees our modern world as having its origin around the year 1000 AD. Someone looking over what is now Europe at that time could not have predicted that a thousand years later it would have the political configuration is now has. 'In 990 nothing about the world of manors, local lords, military raiders, fortified villages, trading towns, city-states, and monasteries foretold a consolidation into the national state.'[29] A thousand years ago, rulers – kings or otherwise – were supposed to subsist on revenues from their own properties and to fund their routine governing activities in the same way. A king might, with the consent of the would-be taxpayers, be allowed to gather revenue for some extraordinary purpose such as a war, but such revenues had to be assented to by those who would bear the burden of them. The English Parliament developed as a body to represent potential taxpayers in considering such extraordinary requests for funding from the King. 'Parliament respected the feudal obligation to give the king what he needed in war, but it reserved the right to decide the extent of royal needs. . . . Parliament claimed the right to decide whether it would pay for wars which sent the king's army across the Channel.'[30] In the development of the modern European state, tax systems have their origin in the state's need for extraordinary revenues. Where the extraordinary was ordinary – where, for example war was more or less permanent, as in Castile during the *reconquista* or in France during the Hundred Years' War – then the taxes were correspondingly permanent; where war was intermittent, the granting of taxes was generally subject to the consent of those about to be taxed either directly or through representative bodies such as parliaments, as in England.

The extraordinary revenues granted to the king in time of war (purportedly for the provision of defence against external aggression) were intended to be once-off subsidies and subject to parliamentary approval. When such approval was not forthcoming 'government used financial expedients: forced loans, borrowing from foreign bankers, currency debasement, and the sale of assets'.[31] War taxes were temporary and conditional; kings wanted them to be permanent and unconditional. The solution? Well, then – let war be perpetual! In France, by the middle of the fifteenth century, given the condition of almost perpetual war in which the country found itself, the once extraordinary taxes had become ordinary; in England, by contrast, extraordinary royal taxes did not escape the watchful eye of Parliament. It is one of history's ironies that when Parliament succeeded in the seventeenth-century struggle between King and Commons, it would give rise to a situation in which the new national executive would be drawn from the ranks of parliamentarians so that there was no longer any real distinction between the tax seekers and the tax approvers and thus no possibility of resistance to the now ordinary extraordinary taxation.[32]

In the end, however, the ever-increasing costs of war steadily eroded the distinction between the extraordinary and the ordinary not just in England but more or less everywhere in Europe. The transition from feudal levies to professional armies connected with the displacement of cavalry and its replacement with massed infantry required substantial financial support: 'the birth of tax systems in Western Europe is tied to this military transition. . . . modern taxation supplanted feudal dues in part because of the need for liquid funds to pay modern standing armies. . . .'[33] Francis Fukuyama notes that the bulk of the budgets of early modern states went on military expenses.

Ninety percent of the budget of the Dutch Republic was spent on war in the period of their long struggle with the Spanish King; 98 percent of the Habsburg Empire's budget went to finance its wars with Turkey and the Protestant powers in the seventeenth century. From the beginning of the seventeenth century to its end, the budget of France rose five- to eightfold, while the British budget increased sixteen-fold from 1590 to 1670. The size of the French army increased proportionately, from 12,000 men in the thirteenth century to 50,000 in the sixteenth, to 150,000 in the 1630s, to 400,000 in Louis XIV's reign.[34]

Remarking on the expansion in the size of bureaucracies, de Jasay writes: 'it has been estimated that over the period from 1850 to 1890 the number of British government employees grew by about 100 per cent and from 1890 to 1950 by another 1000 per cent. . . .' Commensurate with the expansion in the size of the state's bureaucracy was the expansion in the state's budget: 'public expenditure in the nineteenth

century averaged about 13 percent of GNP, after 1920 it never fell
below 24 per cent, after 1946 it was never less than 36 per cent and
in our day it is, of course, just below or just above the halfway mark
depending on how we count public expenditure.'[35] Olwen Hufton
concurs, remarking that armies needed 'massive bureaucracies to
sustain them and that the work of government was directed above
all to ensuring the revenues needful to keep them up and indeed
extend them'.[36] She notes, as we have seen Tilly, Ertman and others
do, that the cost of servicing the debts incurred to pay for the armies
and navies was the really significant element in a state's expenditure,
compared to which, in the early days at least, the state's expenditure
on all other items paled into insignificance.

By the end of the seventeenth century, the king was no longer
merely first among equals but preeminent over all. The ability of
members of the nobility to be a counter-force to the monarch had
more or less vanished for good as they were transformed from quasi-
independent mini-monarchs to courtiers dancing attendance on the
king. The Reformation had effectively eliminated the Church's power
to be an alternative source of authority. In Protestant states, the
church became in effect a government department (and remains so to
some extent even today) and even in Catholic countries it came under
increasing de facto state control.[37]

The making of the modern state and the making of war go hand
in hand, and money, other people's money, lots of it, is required for
both.[38] The king no longer lived off his own but, increasingly, from his
ability to extract resources from a defined territory. It was no longer
possible for a kingdom to be administered personally by a king and his
closest advisers. Expansive and expensive administrative apparatuses,
modelled on those pioneered by the Church as early as the eleventh
century,[39] were established and the tentacles of the state began to
spread into ever more areas. Particularly notable was the attempt to
create a national consciousness by homogenizing language, laws and
customs throughout the various kingdoms.[40] This was a long-term
project that was probably incapable of being realized before the age

of mass communication. As late as the mid-nineteenth century, fewer than half of the people living in the French republic spoke French!

My concern in this book is with the modern state that emerged in the sixteenth and seventeenth centuries in Europe which, while sharing the essential characteristics of all states throughout the ages – a monopolization of allegedly legitimate violence and the coercive extraction of taxes and tributes – has made its own unique contribution to the domination of some by others, in particular, by the invention of bureaucracies employing information and administrative systems that have permitted the modern state to penetrate further and deeper into civil society than could ever have been dreamed of by an Alexander or an Augustus.

The monopoly of violence that characterizes the state can be used in a number of ways. It can be used to wage inter-state wars in which the state is concerned to eliminate (or minimize the influence of) other rival states in struggles over the control of disputed territories; it can be used by the state in its state-making activities to eliminate its internal enemies – rival power blocks or nominally subordinate subjects that constitute possible rivals; it can be used to protect its clients or it can be used to extract the resources to fund its war-making, state-making and protection or wealth-redistribution activities.

Charles Tilly argues that what he calls national states, by which he means 'states governing multiple continuous regions and their cities by means of centralized, differentiated, and autonomous structures'[41] have rarely emerged in early history. Employing this criterion of a national state, most states have been non-national, being 'empires, city-states, or something else'.[42] The highly centralized, differentiated and autonomous state is to all intents and purposes a creature of medieval and modern European history but, although originating in Europe in the relatively recent past, the national state in the twentieth century has become the pattern of the state for all the world. At present, most of the world's surface is, at least nominally, under the control of a host of such states, all built on the modern European model. 'We live in a great age of statebuilding. With the disintegration of the last colonial empires, the second half of this century has witnessed the birth of dozens of new nations in Asia, Africa, and eastern Europe.'[43]

The modern (national) state did not exist prior to 1000 AD. Before that time there were rulers with one title or another and, yes, tribute-taking was a fact of life for the peasantry as it had been from time immemorial but 'It took a long time for national states – relatively centralized, differentiated, and autonomous organizations successfully claiming priority in the use of force within large, continuous, and clearly bounded territories – to dominate the European map.'[44] Indeed, Hufton is of the view that even as late as the eighteenth century, only England, Sweden and Russia among the various contenders for the title of state exhibited the kind and degree of sovereignty that would qualify them for its award.[45]

Not to put too fine a point on it, the modern state came into being by means of what we would now call a protection racket. While it may be worthwhile to pay someone to protect you from real threats or imminent dangers, there is something delightfully quixotic, almost Gilbertian, when the danger or threat from which your protector is protecting you originates primarily or solely from your would-be protector. A classic joke which illustrates this point has it that a man about to be sentenced for the murder of his parents appealed to the judge for mercy on the grounds that he was an orphan. Tilly is uncharacteristically, unacademically blunt when he writes 'To the extent that the threats against which a given government protects its citizens are imaginary or are consequences of its own activities, the government has organized a protection racket.' In terms that could apply to current events, Tilly notes that 'Since governments themselves commonly simulate, stimulate, or even fabricate threats of external war, and since the repressive and extractive activities of governments often constitute the largest threats to the livelihoods of their own citizens, many governments operate in essentially the same ways as racketeers.'[46] When it comes right down to it, there is no moral difference between what pirates, mafia dons and your local friendly bandits do and what the state does – 'banditry, piracy, gangland rivalry, policing, and war making all belong on the same continuum . . .'[47] – the only difference is the claim of legitimacy which cloaks the actions of the state.

In saying what I have just said about the nature and origin of the state, I do not want to be misunderstood. The State is *not* the only source of evil or wrong-doing in the world. There are others, lots of others, and in the end evil finds a ready and welcoming home in the human heart. But the state is unique among wrongdoers in asserting its legitimacy. Your friendly local mugger does not pretend to be doing you a service when he relieves you of your wallet; the chap who steals your TV is not licensed by Thieves Inc. with offices in town, headed notepaper and staff that work from nine to five. As Rothbard pithily expresses it, libertarians regard the state not as the only means by which human beings prey upon each other but as 'the supreme, the eternal, the best organized aggressor against the persons and property of the mass of the public. All States, everywhere . . . '.[48]

The legitimacy of the state

'But', it will be objected, 'to describe the actions of the state as criminal is absurd. The state exercises its power legitimately and its officers are permitted, indeed required, to use violence against some for the good of all whereas criminals and thugs have no right whatsoever to use violence against others.' Everything hinges on this supposed legitimacy of the state, legitimacy being that quality supposedly attached to a state and its actions that makes its use of force and violence ethically acceptable.

As an introduction to the discussion of the legitimacy of the state, I would like to address the double standard that is often used in evaluating the moral quality of state actions in contrast to those of individuals. It is important, in considering ethical and political matters, not to commit the fallacy of misplaced concreteness. We talk of the government or the state as if these were real entities of a different and superior order

of reality from the mundane things we encounter in daily life. But the
government is simply a name for a particular group of people acting,
or being willing to act, in particular ways at a particular time and place.
Such being the case, the presumption must be that they are bound by
the normal rules of conduct that apply to each one of us. With certain
obvious exceptions, what is permissible for one is permissible for the
many; what is impermissible for one is impermissible for the many. As
things stand, I am not allowed to walk up to you and hit you on the nose
just for the fun of it. That action does not become any more permissible
if I do it in conjunction with or at the bidding of others or if I do it to more
than one person. Since the government of a state is simply a group of
people, albeit a group acting under a specific description, it is wrong
for those who constitute the government of a state to do things that
are ethically impermissible to others; 'the great mystery of democracy'
writes Frank van Dun, 'is that "representatives" are vested with powers
that people who empowered them are not and should not be allowed
to exercise'.[49] Libertarians have a unitary conception of the applicability
of moral standards so that the moral value of individuals' actions is the
same whether individuals are acting in their own right or on behalf of a
state.[50] As Rothbard notes, sardonically, 'If you attempted to do to your
neighbours what a democratic government does to its citizens, let us
say, tax them, fix their hours of work, force them to send their children
to schools of your choice, or accept the money you have printed, you
would very likely end up in jail.' And rightly so! 'No democracy allows
you to do such things. Nor does it allow you to undertake these activities
in conspiracy with others. But it does allow you to have someone else
do them in your name and on your behalf!'[51]

If someone wants to make the case for the privileged moral status
of state actors, the burden of proof resides with them. If someone
believes that being a hitman for the Mafia and taking money for killing
to order is wrong, then he is going to have to work hard to show
why being a soldier and doing what appears to be the same thing
(somewhat more efficiently but for rather less money per hit) is right.
Without in any obvious way possessing a different moral status from

ordinary mortals, the people making up the government of the state do things that, if done by anyone else, would be illegal, immoral and criminal – for example, in waging aggressive wars, they murder; in taxing, they steal; in conscripting troops for wars or in imprisoning those who have committed non-aggressive victimless crimes, they kidnap or wrongfully imprison. We read in our histories of men being snatched from city streets and country lanes and forced to serve in the Royal Navy and are shocked at the barbarity of such a practice. But a little reflection will show that the draft laws of the contemporary state are not in any way different in principle from the operations of the press gang; it is just that the naked force of the abducting state is somewhat more muted by the bureaucratic apparatus of the draft board.

When one examines the rhetoric of defenders of the state, one point that comes across with monotonous regularity is the allegedly unique nature of the state that allows it to operate in ways not available to ordinary people.[52] 'Reasons of State' is given as a full and complete justification for actions that we would ordinarily condemn as immoral, or criminal or both. The state is believed to be morally different from you and from me; what you and I cannot do, the state may do with impunity. 'For centuries the State has committed mass murder and called it "war". . . . for centuries the State has enslaved people into its armed battalions and called it "conscription" in the "national service". For centuries the State has robbed people at bayonet point and called it "taxation".'[53] But 'Reasons of State' *cannot* be accepted as a defence for actions that are instances of aggression. As Rothbard points out, 'The distinctive feature of libertarians is that they coolly and uncompromisingly apply the general moral law to people acting in their roles as members of the State apparatus.'[54] And that is precisely the point. Applying the principle of methodological individualism, we can see that there is, properly speaking, no such thing as a state *if* by that we mean an entity ontologically distinct from and superior to ordinary people. The state is simply a name for a particular group of people acting at a particular time in particular ways and the moral law, if it applies to any, applies to all whether they act as agents or principals, on their own behalf or on behalf of others and whether they benefit personally from their actions or not.

> Everyone knows that the State claims and exercises the monopoly of crime . . . and that it makes this monopoly as strict as it can. It forbids private murder, but itself organizes murder on a colossal scale. It punishes private theft, but itself lays unscrupulous hands on anything it wants. . . . Of all crimes that are committed for gain or revenge, there is not one that we have not seen it commit – murder, mayhem, arson, robbery, fraud, criminal collusion, and connivance. . . .[55]

To ground these considerations in your own experience, ask yourself – would *you* allow me to use force against *you* if I disagreed with *your* opinion? Would *you* be prepared to use force against me for the same reason? Would *you* allow me to use violence against *you* to force you to pay for some enterprise *you* objected to? Would *you* be prepared to use violence against me for the same reason? But the state, in the end, is nothing but people such as you and me with perhaps this difference, that politicians 'are normally chosen . . . for their power to impress and enchant the intellectually underprivileged'.[56] It will be said that the state can do what it does only because we empower it to so act. But if you or I cannot do X, we cannot authorize a government to do X. In the principal-agent relationship, we can only delegate to another the powers that we ourselves possess.

The state, then, has different moral standards applied to its actions. How, in fact, does a state get people to obey its edicts? It can do so by the overt use of threats or violence but it is much more effective and inexpensive if it can get people to believe that they have an obligation to obey its commands. This it can do if people are prepared to accept its legitimacy which Antony de Jasay defines as 'the propensity of its [the state's] subjects to obey its commands *in the absence of punishments or rewards for doing so*'.[57]

In order for the state to function, the mass of the people has to believe in its legitimacy.[58] To that end, the state employs a class of professional apologists and controls the means of propaganda, often through dominance of the education system. The task of the State apologist is '. . . to convince the public that what the State does is not . . . crime on a gigantic scale, but something necessary and vital that must be supported and obeyed'.[59] In return for their services, the apologists are rewarded with power and status and allowed to share in the booty obtained from the masses. Chapter 6 of this book is devoted to showing that the legitimacy of the state cannot be justified by recourse to democratic or constitutional theories but here I should like to consider briefly the phenomenon of legitimacy from a psychological and sociological perspective.

We are brought up to believe in the legitimacy of the state: our state-sponsored education confirms us in this belief, everything around us in society supports this belief and nothing appears to count against it.[60] The belief in the legitimacy of the state is all the more effectively planted in the minds of its citizens if it is never actually argued for or justified (that might raise doubts) but simply conveyed inchoately as a foundational principle. As death is regarded as an inescapable fact of natural life, so too does the state and its legitimacy appear to be an inescapable fact of social life. Such is the power of being first in the field – 'positioning' in advertising terms – that the state can literally get away with murder if it can foster the notion that what it does is legitimate. Rothbard claims that the man on the Clapham omnibus, after centuries of propaganda, 'has been imbued with the idea . . . that the government is his legitimate sovereign, and that it would be wicked or mad to refuse to obey its dictates'. The legitimacy of the state has been effectively and insidiously communicated to all by the state's apologists in the churches, the schools, the universities, the press, 'aided and abetted by all the trappings of legitimacy: flags, rituals, ceremonies, awards, constitutions, etc.'[61]

Legitimacy, then, is at least in part a function of the social psychology of particular groups of people conditioned by their historical experience and their individual circumstances. De Jasay remarks that:

> There may be some truth in the belief that some people are more governable than others, so that White Russians, with their reputation for meekness, may have recognized as legitimate, and fairly willingly obeyed, each of the successive and quite different states represented by Lithuanian, Polish and Great Russian rule. On the other hand, people on the Celtic fringes seldom feel that the state deserves their obedience no matter what it does either for them or to them.[62]

As an Irishman, I am naturally inclined to lay de Jasay's flattering unction to my soul but given the extraordinary centralized nature of contemporary Irish political society and the quite spectacular spinelessness of the Irish population under government actions that even in a milder form would have had Frenchmen on the streets in their hundreds of thousands, while I can agree with de Jasay's general point, honesty compels me to reject his remarks on the natural rebelliousness of the Celtic fringe.

Crispin Sartwell makes the interesting claim that the legitimacy defence is in fact a response to the challenge of anarchy. The discovery during the age of exploration of anarchic societies elsewhere in the world provoked intellectual accounts of legitimacy and the dismissal of these anarchic societies as irrational or, at best, not fully rational. 'The sting of the realization that people could exist without the hierarchical instructions of Europe was ameliorated by the idea that such people were, if people at all, savages, or people-as-animals . . . to be an animal is to live in anarchy; to be a civilized human being is to live in thrall to state power.'[63]

The legitimacy of the state gets some support from its close connection with what we might call natural authority. Authority is not merely power; it is, rather, *legitimate* power. In our world, it is widely conceded that parents have authority over their children, employers over their employees, church leaders over their clergy and their adherents, football managers over their players and so on. This kind of authority is endemic in any ordered society. Bertrand de Jouvenal, indeed, claims that 'The phenomenon called authority is at once more ancient and more fundamental than the phenomenon called state; the natural ascendancy of some men over others is the principle of all human organizations and all human advances.'[64] Authority is the capacity, innate or acquired, sometimes embodied in institutions, sometimes not, for exercising ascendancy over groups and individuals and which is perceived as legitimate both by those who exercise it and those who submit to it. If it is not perceived as legitimate, it is not perceived as authority but as force or coercion. Any human group requires some locus of authority – loose and informal, perhaps, but nonetheless real – if it is to function at all. We could, if we wished, call this authority government but it would not be government as that term is employed to refer to what is taken to be the authority of the modern state. The government of the modern state is monopolistic, coercive and it ranges over a clearly specified area and all those who live there. No other form of authority shares this assemblage of characteristics. It is significant that many justifications of political authority have modelled themselves upon what is perhaps the commonest mode of natural authority, namely, the authority of parents over their children. Confucian political thought makes this comparison explicit as does, notoriously, Robert Filmer's justification of royal absolutism in seventeenth century England. But the state is *not* the family writ large, and the relationship of ruler to ruled is *not* that of parent to child.

'But surely! . . .' A preliminary sketch of the argument

The contemporary state does many things. It provides extensive financial support to a large segment of the population (at considerable cost to yet another segment of the population); it organizes and pays for the education (or, at least, the schooling and certification) of the masses from elementary school to university; in many countries, it organizes (after a fashion) and pays for (after another fashion) the health services that most people have access to either at no direct charge to them or at a nominal charge; it provides roads, sewage and refuse services; it regulates business, industry, agriculture and so on. Although the modern state is an enormously large and complicated business, its diverse operations can be grouped together in various ways as displayed in the diagram below.[65] Law and order, justice and defence occupy the centre circle, surrounded by the operations the state engages in to facilitate economic growth, keep inflation low and increase the level of employment. The next circle includes the trinity of health, education and welfare, and the final circle includes public utilities – water, roads and suchlike.

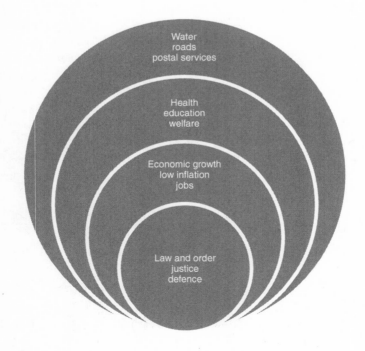

I do not think I am begging the question, or at least not very much, if I suggest that there would appear to be nothing in the nature of the relief of poverty, the provision of education and health, the construction and maintenance of roads, sewage and other utility services that support an argument to the effect that they can *only* be provided by a state. It is at least arguable that the only thing a state can do to improve the economic welfare of its citizens as a whole is to resolutely refuse to interfere in the economy. In the past, many services such as education or transport and roads were provided by private enterprise and some of them are once again being supplied by non-state means. Arguments on most of these matters tend to be practical and come down, in effect, to the question of which way is the best or better way to provide some particular service. Many books and articles on libertarianism discuss these and related matters and you can evaluate the state of these practical questions for yourself. There is, however, one set of functions that is generally regarded as unique to the state and which, it is alleged, cannot be provided at all by any other body: this is the creation, the administration and enforcement of law (the innermost circle in the diagram above).[66] To refute this claim is my principal concern in this book. In the meantime, however, here is a preliminary flavour of some of the objections that immediately arise whenever it is suggested that the state might not be necessary for the tasks of law creation, administration and enforcement.

The objections, in essence, hinge upon the assertion that without the state, there will be disorder, social disharmony, criminality and irresistible attacks on the whole society from inside and from outside. In a stateless world, it is claimed, mutually destructive aggression is unavoidable. Without a coercive monopolistic state to maintain order, long-term stable social relations become difficult, if not impossible, to maintain. The comparative advantage of the strong over the weak will be opportunistically employed to the permanent detriment of the weak. The cost of warding off this aggression will be high, even for the stronger party, and both parties will be worse off than they would be in a situation where aggression is either limited or impossible.[67] That being so, the state is necessary for the production and preservation of order and the maintenance of society.

In the absence of empirical evidence to the contrary, it is an assumption, nothing more, that mutual predation will be the daily fare in a non-state world. Our ordinary experience, however, suggests that human interaction is normally mutually beneficial and that much if not most human interaction is positive-sum rather than zero-sum. Through communication, before, during and after their interactions, people make cost/benefit judgements that are usually accurate and while there will always be some who will seek to benefit from exploiting their greater strength opportunistically, this is a short-term strategy that in the end is likely to be of diminishing utility and, on occasion, even-counter-productive.[68] A little reflection will demonstrate that most of our relations with other people come into being and are maintained outside the ambit of state-generated law and these relations would, for reasons of mutual benefit if for no more elevated reasons, continue in existence and operation even if there were no state to enforce its laws.

Given that the core function of the state is said to be the preservation of law and order and the protection of life and property, it is perhaps not irrelevant to note that recent history shows that most killing has been done by one state or another or by some armed group seeking to be the government of a state and to control its coercive apparatus. The number of people killed in the twentieth century in state-sponsored conflicts or state-related victimization is, at a conservative estimate, between 175,000,000 and 180,000,000.[69] In contrast, although it is impossible to say definitely, the number of people killed in the twentieth century by what we might call normal criminal homicide is nowhere near that number. The figure derived from the same source as that for state-originated deaths gives us roughly 8,000,000 non-state murders worldwide in the twentieth century which is less than 5 per cent of the state-related figure. Matthew White, the author of the source from which these figures derive, appears eager to absolve the state of responsibility for these deaths, remarking 'Governments don't kill people; people kill people.' This, of course, is true but completely misses the essential difference between deadly force employed for personal gain or revenge or hatred and the deadly force employed by agents of states or would-be states in inter- and intra state conflicts. In 1914, the following conversation did *not* take place in a pub in Birmingham, United Kingdom: 'Oh my God, it's deadly boring around here. We need some excitement. I tell you what, lads, let's go to Belgium, live in cold, wet and totally insanitary trenches and shoot at some Germans.' It is undeniable that human beings have killed other human beings for as long as human beings have lived on this planet but to kill other human beings efficiently and in large numbers it takes a state. Given, then, that states have been and are the major agents of death and destruction, their claim to be the necessary agents of the defence and protection of life will delight lovers of irony if being somewhat less amusing to those who have suffered the destruction or their property, injury or death.[70]

The greatness of our historical leaders is built on the mangled bodies of the poor, the defenceless and the politically gullible. Without their ability to dispose of the time, chattels and bodies of the many through the apparatus of the state, our Alexanders, Caesars, Napoleons, Hitlers, Stalins, Clintons, Blairs and Bushes and the innumerable legion of petty tyrants that have plagued the world would have been considerably hampered in their efforts to limit the world's human population. Without these wonderful leaders what would we do for excitement? We would have to be content to live our lives peacefully without witnessing the licensed killing of those less fortunate than ourselves. Harry Lime, in *The Third Man* says '. . . in Italy for 30 years under the Borgias they had warfare, terror, murder, and bloodshed, but they produced Michelangelo, Leonardo da Vinci, and the Renaissance. In Switzerland they had brotherly love – they had 500 years of democracy and peace, and what did that produce? The cuckoo clock!' This comment, of course, is not meant to be complimentary either to Switzerland or to the Swiss but even if there were some truth to it, those who suffered from the warfare, terror, murder and bloodshed of Borgia rule might consider that this was too high a price to pay for some bits of paint on canvas and some nicely chiselled stone.

It is not only in war that the state has been careless with the lives and property of its citizens. Millions of people have lost their lives or their livelihoods as a result of some of the more insane and nightmarish schemes of social engineering attempted by some states in the twentieth century. One has only to recall China's ironically entitled Great Leap Forward, the USSR's disastrous attempts at collectivization, the romantic 'villagizations' of Tanzania, Mozambique and Ethiopia and the killing fields of Cambodia. James Scott believes that these schemes are 'among the great human tragedies of the twentieth century, in terms of lives lost and lives irretrievably disrupted'.[71]

State and society

Much of the inchoate support for the idea of a state results from a conflation of the ideas of state and society. Of course human beings are not isolated individuals; of course we are born in, live in and can only flourish in society where 'society' denotes the sum of the complex, overlapping system of voluntary relations between individuals. But it is a gross mistake to conclude from this that because we need society we therefore need the state. Peter Kropotkin comments that 'man . . . has always lived in societies' but that 'the State is but one of the forms of social life, quite recent as far as regards European societies . . . the centralized State dates but from the sixteenth century'[72] and Rothbard claims that 'The great *non sequitur* committed by defenders of the State, including classical Aristotelian and Thomist philosophers, is to leap from the necessity of *society* to the necessity of the *State*.'[73] Not only is the state not equivalent to society, it is not, properly, even part of society unless we are prepared to recognize criminal gangs as part of society as well: '. . . the State is an inherently illegitimate institution of organized aggression, of organized and regularized crime against the persons and property of its subjects. Rather than necessary to society, it is a profoundly antisocial institution which lives parasitically off the productive activities of its subjects.'[74]

Despite what is widely assumed, state and society are not related as complementary modes of social organization but are in fact competitors. In the matter of power, state and society are engaged in a zero-sum game. What the state gains, society loses; what society gains, the state loses. Society operates on the basis of love or money. People do things for others either because they love them and desire their welfare (as, for example, parents do for their children or lovers do for one another in the first flush of romantic attachment) or they provide services and goods to others in exchange for money. The state, by contrast, relies for its effects on force and coercion.

Finding its role as the preserver of civil order unrewarding, expensive and time-consuming, the state intrudes coercively upon other areas into which it has no business going and in which, we may be thankful, its renowned inefficiency is manifest. In a classic strategy of distraction and displacement, the state, bored with and indifferent to those things for which, allegedly, it primarily exists becomes ever more interested in curtailing and interfering with the lives, liberty and property of its citizens in ways that are more systematically devastating and irresistible than any danger posed by the ordinary criminal. Lovers of the grotesque must surely cherish the irony that the dubiously moral organization known as the state, besides purporting to provide services that are genuinely required (albeit doing so inefficiently and expensively) should also set itself up officiously as the guardian of public morals.

Statelessness does not mean disorganization or imply the disappearance of the need for order. The principles of division of labour and comparative advantage still hold. Under anarchy, suitable enforcement procedures will develop, probably by means of the specialization of existing risk-distribution firms such as insurance companies. In assessing competing solutions to a problem, it is important to consider the merits and demerits of each of the solutions. The benefits of state law enforcement are widely touted. What is not so often adverted to is that when it comes to aggression the state is a much more dangerous aggressor than any band of random criminals. Many of these points will be discussed again throughout the course of the book. Now, however, it is time to take a look at the first of the two key terms in the book's title – libertarianism.

3
LIBERTY AND
LIBERTARIANISM

That libertarianism has something to do with liberty is obvious from its very name; beyond that nominal link, however, things become a little less clear. Libertarianism is a doctrine that, perhaps more than most, is susceptible of being misunderstood or misrepresented. To see what I mean, take a look at 'the 24 types of libertarian' cartoons on the leftycartoon.com site.[1] Here, in 24 panels, we can see a selection of libertarian caricatures depicting, among others, the *naïve libertarian* who thinks that once we get rid of government everything will be alright; the *hypocritical libertarian* who is happy to accept government benefits but is unwilling to pay for them; the *evangelical libertarian*, apostle to the non-libertarian gentiles, who thinks that repeating the mantra 'the market will fix it' is the solution to everything and the '*I did it my way*' *libertarian* who says 'who needs a nanny state? I'll run my own botulism tests!'. While the caricatures are more amusing than either accurate or comprehensible – one panel, for example, seems to suggest that there is something problematic with a libertarian's consistently opposing taxes. Is consistency a vice? – they nevertheless reflect perhaps some of the commonest public (mis)understandings of what libertarianism entails. These (mis)understandings are given some credibility, I regret to say, by the antics of those 'lifestyle' libertarians who teeter on the edge of the abyss of libertinism, if they do not fall right into it, and who appear to be concerned only with garnering the maximum amount of freedom to do whatever they want, regardless of how irritating, offensive or dangerous it may be to others.[2] When he left the Libertarian Party in 1989, the preeminent libertarian of the twentieth century, Murray Rothbard, remarked on the 'general flakiness and counterculturalism of a large section of the LP [Libertarian Party] rank-and-file'.[3] I will have more to say on these matters later on in the chapter but suffice it for now to note that no political theory would stand scrutiny if it were to be judged by the antics of its most bizarre would-be adherents.

The non-aggression principle

Libertarianism is the philosophical and political position that takes as its grounding the fundamental importance of freedom in inter-human relations.[4] From the libertarian perspective, individual freedom forms the context of all mature social relations. The primary social implication of libertarianism is expressed, positively, in the claim that you have the right to do whatever you wish provided only that in so doing you do not infringe on the like right of others. Libertarianism is a politico-economic philosophy of individualism based on the belief that individuals have the unalienable right to live their own lives as they see fit, provided they do not aggress against the equal rights of others. Libertarianism derives its ideas from many sources, including the Austrian School of Economics, Ludwig von Mises, Murray Rothbard, Henry Hazlitt, Walter Block, Hans-Hermann Hoppe and Stephan Kinsella. Other strands from which the Libertarian cloth is woven include the minimal-government American revolutionaries, J. S. Mill, Adam Smith, the classic liberals of the eighteenth and nineteenth centuries, Lysander Spooner, Benjamin Tucker, Frederic Bastiat, Gustave de Molinari and many others.[5]

The limiting condition on the fundamental freedom of human action can be expressed in a negative form in what is sometimes called the non-aggression principle (NAP): *no one may initiate or threaten to initiate the use of coercive physical violence [aggression] against the person or property of another.* It should be noted that what is ruled out by the NAP is the *initiation* of violence (such as murder, rape, theft, assault); libertarianism does *not* rule out the use of violence in *defence* of one's person or property *against* aggression. The practical difficulties of telling the difference in borderline cases between aggression, which libertarianism prohibits, and the forceful resistance of aggression, which libertarianism permits, does not tell against the clear conceptual difference between the two. As part of your fundamental freedom, you have the right to defend your most basic property, yourself, and any other property that you have rightfully acquired. Of course, you may waive that right if you choose so that pacifism and libertarianism are compatible though libertarianism does not require pacifism.

Does adherence to the NAP imply that you must wait until somebody actually physically attacks you before you can respond or that you can never intervene when you believe that some innocent third party is being aggressed against? No. You do not have to wait until someone actually attacks you before you can take steps to defend yourself if, for example, you see them approaching you waving a knife and uttering threats and you believe reasonably that you are in danger. Such knife-waving and threats are themselves the initiation of aggression and you are justified in responding to them accordingly. The common law traditionally made a distinction between assault and battery. Assault was any act that created an apprehension in another of an imminent, harmful or offensive contact, that act consisting of a threat of harm accompanied by an apparent present ability to carry out the threat. Battery, on the other hand, was the actual harmful or offensive touching of another. In the case of innocent others, you can intervene on the side of the putatively aggressed-against, provided you are willing to accept responsibility (moral, criminal and civil) if you get things wrong; if you intervene to defend others against aggression you have to be prepared to be yourself deemed an aggressor if you make a mistake. Prudentially, only if it is manifestly clear that one party is an aggressor and the other aggressed against, should one interfere, and even then it may not always be advisable to do so. These principles hold for groups or organizations as much as for individuals. It is worth noting that George Washington, in his farewell address, cautioned the infant US state against foreign entanglements: 'The great rule of conduct for us in regard to foreign nations is, in extending our commercial relations to have with them as little *political* connection as possible.'[6]

There are some other principles that must be observed in respect of the NAP. Reactive physical violence, even when justified, has to be proportionate to the aggression offered [the proportionality principle] and directed only against the aggressor [the targeting principle]. A moment's reflection will establish this principle. If someone is aggressing against your property by stealing some apples from your orchard, it would be wildly disproportionate, however tempting, to open fire on them with an AK47. In addition, whatever the level of violence one may justifiably use, that violence must be directed only at the aggressor (or his collusive agents) and not against innocent bystanders. One of the appalling consequences of the development of the modern nation state from the seventeenth century onwards has been that where such states are at war, all citizens of a state tend to be judged to be ipso facto contributors to the war effort and, as such, morally and legally indistinguishable from the actual combatants. This appalling doctrine reached its apogee in the twentieth century when cities such as Coventry and Dresden were, as the euphemism goes, 'carpet-bombed' and most shockingly of all in the nuclear destruction of Hiroshima and Nagasaki. The use of some kinds of weapons is clearly incompatible with the targeting principle. Nuclear devices are obviously indiscriminate in their effect, killing and injuring combatants and non-combatants alike and so are fundamentally immoral and unlibertarian but even most 'normal' bombs can only be used in a similarly indiscriminate fashion and such use is also fundamentally immoral and unlibertarian.

From the libertarian perspective, the basic principles of justice apply indifferently to individuals and to groups and there can be no special exemption for states or their agents against moral condemnation, criminal charges or civil actions for acts of aggression. The state and its agents cannot be granted permission to commit actions that everyone would judge to be immoral or illegal if committed by any other person or group in society. It is vital to grasp this point. The idea that there is one law for the individual and another law for the state and its operatives is the root of much of the evil in our world. The transparently obscurantist device of calling violations of justice by euphemistic names (such as taxation or conscription) succeeds only so long as people are willing to be persuaded that using two descriptions for the same phenomenon can make it unjust under one description and just under the other. No one, whether individual, government or state has the right to the James Bond '00' prefix – no one is licensed to kill.

There is something startlingly obvious about the non-aggression principle. As Doug Carkuff[7] points out, we are taught as children not to hit other children and not to take what belongs to them. This is kids' stuff and libertarianism is, in a sense, simply kids' stuff writ large. Obvious the non-aggression principle may be but, when examined, it turns out to rest on a certain conception of property – specifically, it rests on the, perhaps initially startling, claim that we own ourselves and, as the rightful owners of ourselves, only we can rightfully decide what is to be done by and to our bodies and our minds: '. . . what aggression is depends on what our (property) rights are. If you hit me, it is aggression *because* I have a property right in my body. If I take from you the apple you possess, this is trespass – aggression – only *because* you own the apple.'[8] Crispin Sartwell remarks that Locke has an argument to the effect that '. . . if each person is sincere and consistent, they will believe themselves to have inherent rights and will attribute them to others. . . . If someone takes something that I regard as mine, I feel violated'.[9] If people object to this argument, ask them: Do *you* think you should be treated in this way? Do *you* think you are autonomous? What can they say in response?

We do not perhaps normally think of ourselves as something that can be owned but the libertarian self-ownership claim is, at the very least, a rejection of the idea that anyone else owns us. The corollary of owning yourself is that as a free adult person you are also responsible for yourself. No one else is, or can be, obliged to protect, defend, pay for, support, feed, clothe or care for you. Besides owning yourself, you can own and use anything that you rightfully appropriate and which belongs to no one else or anything that you can persuade someone else to transfer to you, whether by sale or gift. For Peter Vallentyne, 'Libertarianism, in the strict sense, is the moral view that agents initially fully own themselves and have certain moral powers to acquire property rights in external things.'[10] You can do what you want with yourself and your property provided that in so doing you do not infringe on the equal rights of others to do what they like with themselves and their properties. This reciprocity is the basis of the only kind of equality that libertarians support: the equality of all individuals before the law – not law as the product of some arbitrary legislative body or other but the natural law towards which all systems of customary law tend and of which they are all, in some measure, an expression.[11]

Libertarianism can be justified either by appeal to consequences – the expansion of the sphere of human liberty will lead to greater prosperity and efficiency – or by appeal to natural law or natural rights – the expansion of the sphere of human liberty is justified by the nature of man and the nature of the world in which he lives. Though the differences between the two approaches may be reconcilable,[12] the approach I take in this book is rights-based rather than consequences-based.

It is important to realize that libertarianism is not, nor is it intended to be, a complete moral theory. Much confusion will be prevented and many possible objections can be summarily deflected if this point is appreciated. To see what the claim that libertarianism is not a complete moral theory means, let me take as a typical example the libertarian attitude towards drugs. Libertarians hold that one should be free to eat, ingest, inject or in any other way introduce into one's body any substance that one chooses. Barring specific contractual obligations and the legitimate exercise of ownership rights, no one else has a right to regulate or prohibit such activity. However, it is one thing to uphold this right to substance-introduction and another thing altogether to recommend or endorse it. Murray Rothbard distinguishes emphatically between a person's right on the one hand and the morality or immorality of the exercise of that right on the other. 'But what may be the moral or immoral ways of exercising that right is a question of personal ethics rather than of political philosophy – which is concerned solely with matters of right, and of the proper or improper exercise of physical violence in human relations.'[13]

Many activities that are currently banned or prohibited by the State – the ingestion of various chemical substances, various forms of consensual sexual congress, contractual relations of various kinds between consenting adults such as prostitution, unrestricted free speech – would all be permissible from a libertarian perspective but not necessarily morally defensible. The libertarian *as libertarian* makes no judgement on the morality of such acts. That such activities should not be legally prohibited does not mean that they are necessarily morally defensible, good, edifying or sensible. Libertarians can and do make moral judgements on many matters but unless the subject matter of those judgements impinges on human freedom, they do so not as libertarians but wearing some other hat.

Given that the state is the principal (but not the only) threat to liberty, some libertarians of an anarchist stripe would like to see the end of the state as a whole. Other libertarians (minarchists) would be satisfied with a drastic reduction in its size and scope and its restriction to what they would regard as its core ineliminable functions of defence against external aggression and the maintenance of internal order. Whatever the outcome of the dispute between anarchists and minarchists, all libertarians, who as libertarians are emphatically *not* opposed to order, can accept any form of governance provided that it is arrived at freely and consensually.

Reciprocity

Why should the NAP be respected? Because transgressing this principle results in the violation of the basic liberty of other people, their liberty to dispose of themselves and their lawfully acquired property as they see fit. An unwillingness to accept and abide by this principle requires one either to defend a radically implausible form of special pleading ('I am special so that I may infringe upon the liberty of others but they must respect mine') or to be prepared to concede to others the right to violate one's own liberty, a concession that is not without its own costs. Crispin Sartwell concretizes the argument by appealing directly to the sensibilities of the reader. It is not easy to find people who are prepared to admit that they could legitimately have their freedom arbitrarily restricted by another. 'Whatever your notion of rights, I hope that you feel that there ought to be some zone of autonomy around yourself, and that when you yourself are used as a mere tool or device for some other person, some important principle or reality is being violated or denied.'[14] And if you are willing to maintain that, then how can you not consider that the same holds true for everyone else. 'I do not want to be tortured. I assume that you feel the same. And if you do, then I ask you to join me in condemning torture when it is performed on people other than ourselves as well.'[15]

The golden rule is the essence of all systems of ethics and justice and is based on a principle of reciprocity.[16] Recognizing the fundamental ontological and ethical equality of all human beings, I accept the obligation to treat others as I myself want to be treated. The golden rule emerges spontaneously from the practices of peaceful human social interchange, and its apprehension, fitful and intermittent though it may be, marks the transition in each individual's life from the natural and utilitarian levels (which we never quite leave behind) to the truly moral. The ethical systems of all the major world religions and cultures converge on this principle. The ethical differences that appear between cultures are largely due to material factors, to limitations that arise from historical circumstances and that prevent some or all in a community from seeing the truly universal nature of the golden rule or prevent its application to all.

The golden rule comes in two versions: positive – do unto others as you would have them do unto you, and negative – do not do unto others as you would not have them do unto you. Cicero writes 'The primary function of justice is to ensure that no one harms his neighbour unless he has himself been unjustly attacked.'[17] While libertarianism springs unproblematically from the negative version of the rule, its positive version can be problematic. If it is incorporated unalloyed as an element into the legal order then some will be required by law to do things for others (outside the realm of contract) and thus their freedom will be compromised. Of course, as already mentioned, the libertarian principles are not the only principles we can adopt and there is nothing to stop us from freely adopting the positive version of the golden rule – perhaps from religious or humanitarian convictions – but this, of course, is quite compatible with libertarianism since no one else is coercing us so to choose.

Freedom is essential to human flourishing. To be free is to be protected against aggression and coercion and in that happy state, to be able to make and pursue plans.[18] Why is freedom important? Surely it is not the only human good? No, it is not the only human good; it is, however, the foundation of all the other goods. 'Coercing people', writes Sartwell, 'reduces the moral content of their lives, reduces them to the status of inanimate objects. To seek systematically to reduce the scope of freedom, however freedom is to be understood metaphysically, is to attack the status of human beings as moral agents'.[19] To be human is to be able to act and for action to be genuine it must be free. If we are to be able to flourish, then, we must be free to make our choices, for good or for ill. The only limitation on our freedom of action is the requirement to respect the other's freedom of action. Human flourishing is linked to the development of the virtues and the development of the virtues presupposes freedom.

Libertarians believe that liberty must be the default position for any ethical or political theory. Any attempt to justify liberty makes it a derivative from some other principle and so not fundamental.[20] Liberty is a constitutive (not merely instrumental) aspect of human existence and human action and unless there are specific reasons to restrict it (such as a person's using it for the purposes of aggression against others) liberty cannot be compromised. If liberty is to be restricted, the burden of proof is on those who would restrict it, not on those who would defend it.[21]

Libertarian liberty is not formless in a Sartrean sort of way. If we are truly free, then that freedom permits us to bind ourselves. In what might appear as a paradox, unless we are free to bind ourselves we are not truly free! We can, therefore, sell our labour, our times, our products, commit to be and to do things for shorter or longer periods and even for life. In a word, we can contract. Without this ability to self-bind, it is difficult to see how our liberty could be utilized to increase our welfare.

As a political theory, libertarianism is the reflective appropriation and expression of the centrality of liberty to a properly human life. As already stated, libertarianism is not (and is not intended to be) a complete moral theory. The use of freedom to follow one's desires regardless of the welfare of others is to be a libertine and libertarianism is not libertinism. Libertarianism puts minimal conditions on the exercise of freedom, again based on the principle of reciprocity, to the effect that one may do whatever one wishes provided only that in so doing one does not aggress against another. A society built solely on libertarian principles would be just but there can be few libertarians who would see libertarian principles as the end of a complete human life and not just as the minimal preconditions for such a life. Most societies encourage self-restraint beyond the basic limits set by libertarianism and such self-restraint is the basis of artistic, musical and ethical culture and, via delayed gratification, of economic development by means of the capital that such delayed gratification produces.

Besides the cooperation and competition that is the warp and woof of normal human living, there is always the possibility that some in a society will attempt to aggress against others, that is, to initiate the use of force. To prevent or minimize this aggression and to restore the status quo ante, societies develop customary laws. As with ethics, language, money, logic and other important constituents of human life, customary laws develop spontaneously from the matrix of social life. The basic principle underlying it is the principle of reciprocity. This topic is the subject of Chapter 5.

Aggression is not merely harm

In his otherwise excellent book, Crispin Sartwell adopts a quasi-Hayekian account of aggression that places it on a continuum ranging from naked force at one end to nagging at the other.[22] This will not do. Pointing a gun at someone's head and demanding that he open the bank vault or else is clearly aggression; nagging someone, however unpleasant that nagging may be, is not. There will be the usual boundary issues arising from problematic cases but that does not prevent us from distinguishing acts that are clearly aggressive from acts that are clearly not aggressive. As an instance of aggression, Sartwell instances blackmail. Here, I would have to say in agreement with Walter Block, that however morally repugnant or harmful blackmail might be, unless it is accompanied by force or threats of force, it is not in itself aggression.[23] It is not just the fact that someone attempts to bend me to his will that makes an action aggressive; the means employed are crucial.

The fatal ambiguity between injustice (resulting from aggression) and harm (resulting from the human condition) derives ultimately from J. S. Mill's *On Liberty*. The notion of harm in Mill's essay is systematically ambiguous as is evidenced by his use of a range of near-synonyms ('evil', 'injury', 'damage', 'hurt', 'concern', 'affect', 'regard' and 'molest') in his application of the principle. These near-synonyms fall into two broad classes: the neutral – 'concern', 'affect' and 'regard' – and the negative – 'hurt', 'damage', 'injury' and 'evil'. Since, however, it can be argued that everything everybody does concerns, affects or regards another in some way or other, however trivial, the seemingly neutral terms employed by Mill must be understood in a negative way if his principle is not to become vacuous. In a word, those actions that concern, affect or regard others, must affect or regard them in a harmful fashion. Shoehorning 'harm' or its equivalent into the meaning of the neutral concepts employed by Mill, while necessary, is still not sufficient to avoid every difficulty. If Algernon takes the last cucumber sandwich before Jack can get to it, or if Tom buys the last seat for the opera as Harry stands fretting behind him in the ticket queue, Jack and Harry have been harmed. Even so, it is difficult to see how anyone could censure the actions of Algernon or Tom unless there is some other element of their conduct that is otherwise objectionable. Towards the end of his essay, and somewhat belatedly, Mill recognizes the point that an action that negatively affects the interests of another does not necessarily justify intervention by society. 'Whoever succeeds in an overcrowded profession or in a competitive examination, whoever is preferred to another in any context for an object which both desire, reaps benefit from the loss of others, from their wasted exertion and their disappointment' but 'society admits no right, either legal or moral, in the disappointed competitors to immunity from this kind of suffering'.[24]

Getting serious

Philosophers and the explanations they give must be serious.[25] Being serious does not mean that we have to be solemn or portentous – we can be serious and humorous, just as we can be frivolous and pedantic – but a condition of holding a belief, *really* holding that belief rather than just notionally adhering to it, is that our actions should, as far as possible, conform to it. At the very least, if we are serious, there should be no gratuitous contradiction between what we claim to believe and the actions we perform. It is possible that a contradiction of a certain kind may arise between certain kinds of belief and the serious assertion of those beliefs. We might put this in the form of the following maxim:

> ***M****: No theory can be seriously maintained such that, if it were to be true, its very maintenance would become impossible, meaningless, contradictory or self-refuting.*

Apart from the formal constraints on theories of the necessity for consistency and coherence, and the material constraints of explanatory adequacy and coverage, there is also a self-referential constraint on theories, namely that theories must not render impossible the conditions of their own statement or the conditions of their being maintained. If they do so, they are theoretically self-stultifying.

Unless human beings are fundamentally free in their choices and decisions, it is not possible for statements to be meaningfully asserted, and that includes the statement of a radical determinism or a radical irrationalism. The statement of a radical determinism is undermined by its own content's rendering pointless the act of its assertion or by its assertion's rendering meaningless the content of that assertion; the same holds true for the statement of a radical irrationalism. Iris Murdoch writes, 'As a philosophical theory, as contrasted with a theological view or an assumption of popular science or an emotional intuition about fate, *determinism fails because it is unstateable.*' And just as no matter how far you track a movie camera backwards, it can never itself be directly in shot, so too, 'However far we impinge (for instance for legal or moral purposes) upon the area of free will we cannot philosophically exhibit a situation in which, instead of shifting, it vanishes. *The phenomena of rationality and morality are involved in the very attempt to banish them.*'[26] Strict determinism falls foul of **M** since, of necessity, the very attempt to argue for determinism is itself a free act by the arguer that commends itself to the rational judgement of its intended audience. If it is not a free act, we need not regard it; it is only the sighing of the breeze in the vocal chords of the determinist.

Darwin wrote to a correspondent whose book he was reading, 'you have expressed my inward conviction . . . that the Universe is not the result of chance'. But then, in a remark intended to cast doubt on his own inward conviction that the universe is not the result of chance, he makes a dialectical move that, if successful, would poison all the wells of rationality. '[W]ith me', he writes, 'the horrid doubt always arises whether the convictions of man's mind, which has been developed from the mind of the lower animals, are of any value or at all trustworthy'. And in a question that one might have expected to issue from the mouth of Bishop Wilberforce rather than the author of *The Origin of Species*, he asks: 'Would any one trust in the convictions of a monkey's mind, if there are any convictions in such a mind?'[27]

In fact, the implicit argument embodied in **M** can be marshalled against all forms of eliminative materialism or, more generally, all forms of reductive naturalism. It is hard to disagree with Lynne Rudder Baker when she says that, 'To deny the common-sense conception of the mental is to abandon all our familiar resources for making sense of any claim, including the denial of the common-sense conception.' She continues, 'If the thesis denying the common-sense conception is true, then the concepts of rational acceptability, of assertion, of cognitive error, even of truth and falsity are called into question.'[28]

Our lives as philosophers cannot be radically divorced from what we do when we are not doing philosophy. In a normal day, we go to work, read and answer our mail, teach our students, work on papers or books, go to meetings, have lunch, make small talk with acquaintances, discuss last night's football game and so on, all of which actions are shot through with purpose and intentionality. In our non-philosophical dealings with our families, friends and colleagues, we treat them as rational moral agents, as people responsible for their actions, sometimes praising them, more often, alas, blaming them, but always morally evaluating their actions. We assume, without any difficulty, the reality of the ethical dimension of our lives and the lives of others and the appropriateness of moral judgement. But moral judgements make sense only if human actions are significantly free. Freedom, in turn, if it is possible at all, is co-implicative with rationality such that only the free can be rational and only the rational can be free.

At this point, some readers may echo the sentiment of Colonel Pickering in *My Fair Lady*, who objects to Professor Higgins' criticism of Eliza's way of speaking with 'Come, sir, I think you picked a poor example!' Perhaps I have, but when one strips away the veneer of sophistication surrounding reductionist accounts of human action, they all suffer from the same principled problem. It is just not possible to reconcile the intentionalistic and purposive act of producing a reductionist account with the fact that reductionism itself undermines the very possibility of that account's actually meaning something.

Determinism, whether psychological, theological or metaphysical, undermines freedom and morality. Those who preach determinism, if they are to be taken seriously, must be prepared to live by that doctrine. But determinism is impossible to live out practically and so cannot be a serious philosophical position. Illness, disease, passion and exhaustion may make inroads into our freedom but they cannot totally eliminate it; if they could do so it would be at the cost of making us cease to be human. In a similar way, fundamental attacks on human rationality are similarly destructive of morality. If they are to be taken seriously, those who preach irrationalism – whether in the form of deconstructionism, perspectivalism, postmodernism or polylogism – must live by those doctrines. There is little point in discussing the respective merits of an ethics of duty, let us say, as against consequentialism or against virtue ethics if at any moment someone can pull the rug out from under the entire discussion by questioning the very possibility of ethics in the first place. The best, perhaps the only, way to demonstrate the non-viability of determinism and irrationalism is by means of the self-stultifying argument. Those who deny the reality of human liberty or deny its fundamental importance to there being any value in human life, considered either individually or together in society, cannot be taken seriously.

Libertarianism and conservatism[29]

Libertarianism is often conflated with conservatism. Many people think that libertarianism is simply a more radical or cruder version of conservatism. Perhaps because of this, and despite the common elements in both their names, libertarianism is much less likely to be conflated with liberalism. Liberalism and conservatism are often represented by a simple line, with liberalism to the left of its centre and conservatism to its right. Attempts to locate libertarianism on this line are misguided and likely to result in an impression that libertarianism has a sort of politically split personality inasmuch as it will be located squarely on the left on some issues such as being anti-war and supporting pro-civil liberties, and sitting solidly on the right on other issues such as favouring laissez faire economics and rejecting legally mandated equality laws. From the libertarian point of view, conservatives differ from liberals only in that they wish to use the apparatus of state power to enforce their moral or religious views rather than their economic views on others. Libertarianism, then, undercuts the validity of the one-dimensional liberal–conservative model of political positions.

If we take a look at some practical policy issues it is difficult to see how people could think conservatism and libertarianism are essentially the same. Conservatives believe in limited government, private property, free markets and individual liberty *except for* state-controlled social security and social welfare, state-funded and state-controlled healthcare, state prohibitions on the manufacture, exchange and use of certain drugs, state-enforced, state-funded and state-controlled public schooling, state-generated and enforced economic regulations, state-generated minimum-wage laws and price controls, state-produced fiat currencies, state-levied income taxes, state-arranged trade restrictions, state-imposed immigration controls, state-produced monopolies (such as the postal service), state-controlled foreign aid, state-sponsored wars of aggression and foreign occupations, standing armies, a military-industrial-banking-state complex, ever-increasing infringements on civil liberties by the state and its agencies and out-of-control state spending funded by confiscatory taxation and monetary inflation to pay for all this. Libertarians, on the other hand, believe in individual liberty, free markets, private property and limited government. *No exceptions.*[30] Libertarian critics of conservatism do not have it all their own way in the polemical department. The well-known conservative writer Russell

Kirk has his own characterization of libertarianism.[31] Apart from their common detestation of collectivism and governments that go beyond their competence, Kirk believes that conservatives and libertarians have little or nothing in common.

One topic on which libertarians and conservatives disagree is that of the importance of liberty. Conservatives are not opposed to liberty as such. Liberty is valuable but, given the conservative commitment to order, it must be subordinated to morality and to traditional social norms. Libertarians, by definition, value individual liberty in a special way. They reject the imposition by force of particular conceptions of virtue, justice and the good society that, whatever value they may have, do not justify the forcible invasion of a person's freedom. Libertarianism concerns itself only with determining the conditions in which force or the threat of force may legitimately be used in human relations, namely, for the protection of human individual liberty; all other employments of force or the threat of force are illegitimate: '. . . libertarianism is a claim about the scope of permissible force or the threat of force among human beings, including human beings who constitute the governing administration of a given human community.'[32]

It is clear that conservatives and libertarians accord liberty different priorities. Robert Nisbet claims that for libertarians 'individual freedom, in almost every conceivable domain, is the *highest of all social values*' and is so 'irrespective of what forms and levels of moral, aesthetic, and spiritual debasement may prove to be the unintended consequence of such freedom'.[33] This is an instructive, if question-begging, judgement. On the contrary, I should say that for libertarians, liberty is the *lowest* of social values, lowest in the sense of being most fundamental, a *sine qua non* of a human action's being susceptible of moral evaluation in any way at all. Human freedom can be used for all sorts of actions directed to all sorts of purposes that are then susceptible to moral evaluation, but unless human action is free from coercion moral evaluation is intrinsically impossible. Libertarians value freedom as a hard core basic value without which morally significant human action is simply not possible, but while libertarianism as such has nothing to say beyond asserting and defending individual liberty this is not at all the same as thinking that libertarians in living out their lives are concerned with nothing other than liberty. This would be as absurd as to think that someone who insisted on the absolute necessity of water for human survival should be taken to assert that water was the only thing needed for a rich and interesting diet! As if to contradict Nisbet, Murray Rothbard, whose credentials as a libertarian none can doubt, remarked that 'Only an imbecile could ever hold that freedom is the highest or indeed the only principle or end of life.' For him, such a claim is scarcely coherent or meaningful. He agreed with Lord Acton that 'freedom is the highest *political* end, not the highest end of man per se . . .'.[34]

It cannot be too heavily emphasized that the limited, although potent, scope of libertarianism is not intended to deny the importance of love, community, discipline, order, learning or any of the many other values that are essential to human flourishing. Libertarians can cherish these values as much as anyone else but, however much they might cherish them, they reject any and all attempts to produce them by force, coercion or intimidation. They regard such attempts at coercion as both wrong in themselves and as ineffective. As Tibor Machan puts it, 'force is permissible and useful only in repelling force, not in building character, love, faith, scientific knowledge, etc.'[35] In the end, the question for the libertarian is this: 'Should virtuous action (however we define it) be compelled, or should it be left up to the free and voluntary choice of the individual?'[36] No third road is possible here; one must choose compulsion or liberty. And if compulsion is the conservative's choice, then a further embarrassing question awaits him: who will do the compelling? Our political masters? If recent history has taught us anything (and history teaches us many lessons that we never seem to learn) it is that our erstwhile political superiors are rarely our moral superiors and are, given the grubby nature of practical politics, very often our moral inferiors.

Libertarianism then while it makes no claim to comprehend a total moral framework, is not antagonistic to such a framework. One of the reasons, historically, why libertarians generally prefer to avoid the topic of virtue is not that they are intrinsically opposed to it but because the promotion of virtue has often been used as an excuse to legitimize coercion. All too many conservatives (and, indeed, liberals) are keen to use the power of the state to enforce their particular vision of the human good so that '. . . people may be forced to do what needs to be done to achieve the good'. For the conservative, 'it is the state of having *reached* the end that is morally relevant, not the process of having lived *by seeking it* or some other self-perfecting approach' and, as Machan wryly notes, 'This view has been devastating in the modern age.'[37] One way of understanding the difference between conservatives and libertarians is that conservatives are relatively more concerned about the achievement of the ends than about the process by which the ends are achieved whereas libertarians are concerned as much with the process as with the ends themselves.

Misunderstandings can arise from a failure to recognize the severely limited ethical scope of libertarianism. At the risk of repeating myself, it must be clearly understood that libertarianism does *not* imply that all modes of conduct are equally valuable or have equal merit. There may well be those who think of themselves as libertarians who think this, but such a view, despite Kirk's assertion that liberty descends into a maelstrom of licence, is not a necessary consequence of libertarianism as such. A libertarian may choose to be a libertine but there is nothing in libertarianism to constrain him to be one. Machan asks, 'Is libertinism implicit in the advocacy of liberty as the highest political principle?' and he answers, 'No – libertarianism only prohibits the forceable quelching of indecent conduct, not its vigorous criticism, opposition, boycott or denunciation in peaceful ways.'[38] Libertarianism is compatible with a whole variety of ethical positions – virtue ethics, an ethics of duty, even consequentialism. Libertarians can and do disagree about which of these ethical positions is most compatible with libertarianism but this is a family quarrel *within* libertarianism. Any system of morality or politics that does not infringe upon individual liberty is acceptable to libertarianism; any system that infringes upon individual liberty is not. Many of the conservative's criticisms of libertarianism are really criticisms of the utilitarian consequentialism of classical liberalism, but although libertarianism may overlap at some points with classical liberalism it must not be conflated with it. To the extent that libertarians are prepared to accept the state (and many are not), it is to be regarded as the agency that helps to maintain the order of the social nexus in which individuals interact. The promotion of virtue is *not* and cannot be the primary task of the state, although in preserving liberty (as it is alleged to do) where liberty is a precondition of all moral action the state may contribute indirectly to the promotion of virtue.

Is libertarianism utopian?

Libertarianism is often criticized for having a naively optimistic view of human nature.[39] In fact, if anything, it is the modern liberal who has a utopian conception of human perfectibility while the modern conservative inclines towards a quasi-Calvinistic concept of our inherent and radical sinfulness. The libertarian is committed to neither of these extremes. Some people are good; some are not. Some good people sometimes behave badly; some bad people sometimes behave well. While libertarians are committed to neither optimism nor pessimism regarding human nature, they *are* committed to the proposition that coercion in respect of matters such as social practices, sexual habits, religious beliefs and political allegiances violates human nature. But, of course, coercion is not the only tool in the box for the achievement of social goals. The exercise of parental authority may come close to coercion but can be justified if exercised reasonably in fulfilment of a kind of trusteeship over those not yet capable of making fully adult choices. Ostracism, boycott, exclusion, vocal disapproval, termination of friendships, expulsion from voluntary groups are all non-coercive and effective means of modifying social behaviour that can be used always and everywhere without violating the basic libertarian commitment to freedom.

Libertarianism is consistent with any theory of human nature provided that the theory does not either explicitly or implicitly deny the significance of human freedom. Machan, for one, sees Aristotelianism as the broader framework within which libertarianism can operate where Aristotelianism comprises a kind of metaphysical pluralism, the view that reality manifests itself in many different ways. Consistent with this pluralism is a monism of principles. With the emergence of life, objective values also emerge. We can choose to live or choose to die. We can choose to live well or to live badly. For Machan, libertarianism is a political theory that best takes into account man's nature, 'his essence as a free, rational living being whose conduct can only be made morally worthwhile by the individual himself by sustaining his commitment'.[40] The good human life aims at a whole range of virtues, none of which can be achieved unless man is free to choose them.

Libertarianism differentiates itself from liberalism (in both its classic and its modern incarnations) and also from conservatism in rejecting the use of force in all cases except those of resisting or punishing aggression. The modern liberal is (or was, until recently) content to use the power of the state to enforce his economic views on all to produce what he considers to be the correct distribution of goods and services while claiming as large a space as possible for personal, especially sexual, morality; the conservative, on the other hand, generally wishes to leave as much space as possible for economic activities while recruiting the state to enforce his moral views on others. Unlike the libertarian for whom liberty operates as a principle across the whole range of human endeavour, both the liberal and the conservative are selective in those spheres in which they will allow liberty to operate. Where a libertarian differs from the conservative in the matter of custom, habit and tradition is not necessarily in his lack of appreciation of their social, moral and cultural value but simply in refusing to allow their maintenance or propagation by means of force or coercion. If coercion is ruled out, then many libertarians are only too willing to entertain a presumption in their favour.

The libertarian relies on a sharp distinction between the realm of morality and the realm of legality. Legality is determined by considerations of justice and justice, in turn, is a function of non-aggression. Whatever is done, provided it involves no aggression or threat of aggression, is ipso facto just; it is not, however, ipso facto moral. Rothbard distinguishes emphatically between 'a man's *right* and the morality or immorality of his exercise of that right'.[41] The possession of a right is one thing, its exercise is quite another. The moral or immoral ways of exercising that right 'is a question of personal ethics rather than of political philosophy' whereas political philosophy is concerned 'solely with matters of right, and of the proper or improper exercise of physical violence in human relations'.[42] It can hardly be said too often or too bluntly that, despite the suspicions of Kirk and others, libertarianism is *not* the same thing as libertinism. Libertarianism will not admit the physical restraint or physical punishment of acts that do not aggress against others but it nowhere implies moral approval of such acts or rules out their restraint by other methods. If libertarianism disconnected from the customs and traditions dear to conservatism runs the risk of becoming a mere fleshless skeleton, conservatism without the principled core of libertarianism risks being unable to differentiate between that which is genuinely fulfilling and perfective of human nature and the merely customary, transient and contingent.

In sum, libertarianism has one and only one basic principle – that all should be free to do whatever they wish to do provided only that in so doing they do not aggress against others. This principle is both simple and initially attractive; what is not quite so simple or attractive (at least to the conservatives) is its consequences. When conservatives realize what these consequences are they tend to have second thoughts about the principle. H. L. Mencken thought that liberty was too strong a drink for many people and that what they really wanted was security. What tends to divide libertarians from conservatives is the conservatives' failure to realize or unwillingness to concede that toleration is not equivalent to endorsement. It should be obvious (but apparently it is not) that to tolerate something is not the same thing as to approve of it. If toleration required approval, toleration would not be a virtue. What value is there is being prepared to tolerate only those things of which you approve? The libertarian may adopt any of a number of moral attitudes towards various issues – drugs, prostitution and so on – but the only question for him as a libertarian is not whether these modes of activity are to be commended or are a fitting mode of human activity taken in the round, but only whether in engaging in such activities a person is infringing on the liberty of another. If the answer to this question is no then this mode of activity cannot be coercively prohibited however much it may be disapproved of. Of course, in a society constructed on libertarian principles you have the right to license or to refuse to license whatever behaviour you choose on your own property provided, of course, you are prepared to accept the economic and social consequences if other people disapprove of your licensing arrangements. It would follow, therefore, that in such a society one would be within one's rights (however inexpedient it might otherwise be to do so) to prohibit types of behaviour of which one morally disapproved to licensees on one's property on pain of the withdrawal of the licence, just as one is entitled to require a visitor to one's home to leave if his behaviour should become unacceptable or for any other reason whatsoever or for none. Such a right subsists whether a property is owned by one person or by a whole community. In such a way, then, but only in such a way, could conservative principles obtain traction in a libertarian society.

4
ANARCHY AND ANARCHISM

At the heart of the idea of anarchy is a deep-rooted resistance to having your life and actions ordered by others to whom you have not voluntarily subordinated yourself. As with most interesting ideas, the idea of anarchism is controversial.[1] For reasons mainly historical, anarchism has perhaps been most associated with socialist or quasi-socialist movements[2] so that D. Novak can say that, 'anarchism is opposed to private ownership of land and capital'.[3] If this is so, then the term *cannot* be used by those who are not opposed to private ownership of natural resources or capital and that would be a problem for me and for other libertarian anarchists for whom the ownership of property is a key element in the realization of our freedom in the world.

A matter of definition

There are many futile activities and pursuits in this world of ours – state central planning and herding mice at crossroads are two that immediately spring to mind – but ranking high in the futility charts must be verbal disputes about whether or not a hotly contested concept 'really' applies to this or that phenomenon. 'Is this *really* art?' we ask, with a heavy emphasis on the 'really', attempting to smuggle in a judgement ('It's not very good, is it?') under the guise of a neutral classification. The concept of anarchy is one such highly contested concept and many who identify themselves as anarchists are unwilling to allow others to describe themselves as such. '*We* are really anarchists', they say, '*you* are not!'[4] It is true that unless you want to end up talking to yourself like Humpty-Dumpty in *Through the Looking Glass*[5] a term cannot be used to mean something completely at odds with its normal range of uses but neither is it the case that words are a kind of trademark that some groups have an exclusive right to use and others do not. Noam Chomsky remarks that 'No one owns the term "anarchism." It is used for a wide range of different currents of thought and action, varying widely.'[6]

In the case of 'anarchism', its range of appropriate uses is, despite some protestations to the contrary, given by any good dictionary. The *Oxford English Dictionary* tells us that 'anarchy' derives from the Greek privative prefix *'an'* together with *'archos'* meaning a leader or chief. It thus comes to have a root meaning of absence of government with, in its popular signification, the additional idea of lawlessness or disorder resulting from that absence (notice the tacit assumption that without the guiding hand of the government, we would all be at one another's throats). Anarchy can also, if more rarely, signify a state of society without government without any additional implication that the absence of government necessarily spells disorder. Somewhat more rarely still, it can signify the absence or non-recognition of authority and order in any sphere whatsoever, for example, in morals or religion, and not only in society at large.

Although anarchism is typically taken to be a doctrine that characteristically rejects the domination of people by the state, it should perhaps rather be *formally* defined as the rejection of *any* form of non-voluntary domination of one person or group of people by another. If this is how anarchism were to be defined, then it would be an open question as to what modes of human interaction *materially* exemplify this non-voluntary domination. The commonest example of non-voluntary domination is, of course, the state but it may not be the only one. Anarchists on the communist and collectivist end of the political spectrum believe that the institution of private property necessarily gives rise to non-voluntary domination, as does the relationship of employer to employee. Since I believe we are free to bind ourselves by entering into informal and contractual relations with others, even relations in which we voluntarily subordinate ourselves to others, I do not accept the common claim of anarchists from the left side of the political spectrum that such relations are necessarily anti-anarchic. If we are not free to bind ourselves then we are not really free; our liberty is compromised. The form of anarchism that accepts this radical notion of freedom, our freedom to bind ourselves, I call libertarian anarchism.[7]

The term 'anarcho-capitalism' is used by some to name the position I am defending here. Some anarchists will say that anarcho-capitalism cannot be anarchism because capitalism and the state are inextricably linked (the first giving rise to the second or vice versa) or because capitalism necessarily exhibits coercive hierarchical structures such as that between employer and employee. If the term 'anarchy' is troublesome the term 'capitalism' is scarcely less so. 'Capitalism' carries so much emotional and conceptually confusing baggage, either positive or negative depending on your point of view, that it can scarcely be used in a neutral descriptive way. Noam Chomsky was once asked what he thought of anarcho-capitalism and despite conceding that he agreed with anarcho-capitalists on a range of issues, appreciated their willingness to publish his material when no one else would and being complimentary about their commitment to rationality, he said that a society foolish enough to allow its implementation would be destroyed. 'Anarcho-capitalism . . . is a doctrinal system which, if ever implemented, would lead to forms of tyranny and oppression that have few counterparts in human history. . . . The idea of "free contract" between the potentate and his starving subject is a sick joke. . . .'[8]

Murray Rothbard tried to make conceptual space for the term 'anarcho-capitalism' by distinguishing two different kinds of capitalism, remarking that 'the term "capitalism" was coined by its greatest and most famous enemy, Karl Marx' but that 'what Marx and later writers have done is to lump together two extremely different and even contradictory concepts and actions under the same portmanteau term'. These contradictory concepts Rothbard styles 'free-market capitalism' and 'state capitalism' and the difference between them is 'precisely the difference between, on the one hand, peaceful, voluntary exchange, and on the other, violent expropriation'.[9]

David Osterfeld makes essentially the same point when he distinguishes between economic capitalism and sociological capitalism. Economic capitalism signifies 'production according to the dictates of the market' whereas sociological capitalism 'is defined in terms of . . . the ownership of the means of production by the 'bourgeois', or ruling class'.[10] Sociological capitalism finds expression in reality as what is often called 'mercantilism', the incestuous relationship between big business, banking and government, a position that has been vehemently excoriated by libertarians in both its historic and in its current manifestations. Free market defenders of capitalism generally have economic capitalism in mind when they defend capitalism (at least they should have) though it must be conceded that sometimes a little carelessness creeps in and the mercantilist status quo becomes the object of defence. In truth, however, not only are libertarian anarchists *not* committed to a defence of sociological capitalism, they are, in fact, resolutely opposed to it. Needless to say, failure to keep these two very different accounts of capitalism apart has led to much confusion and 'critics and opponents of capitalism talked past each other when many were in basic agreement'.[11] Of one mind on this point with both Rothbard and Osterfeld, Walter Block distinguishes between corporate state monopoly capitalism and anarcho- or laissez faire capitalism and remarks that 'these two systems are as different as night and day. They have nothing in common except for this highly unfortunate terminology that labels both "capitalism"'.[12] The positions I take in this book are likely to be controversial enough without my running the risk of being taken to defend what I do not in fact defend, namely, the idea that capitalism *as mercantilism* is desirable from a libertarian anarchist perspective. I not only do *not* want to defend mercantilism, I want to highlight the radical sociopolitical implications of my conception of liberty. For these reasons, despite Rothbard's and Osterfeld's and Block's commendable attempts to draw and maintain a defensible distinction between two kinds of capitalism, I am going to describe my position not as anarcho-capitalism but as libertarian anarchism.[13]

The libertarian anarchist has to be prepared to tolerate whatever arrangements may be arrived at by particular social groups provided only that no coercion is used on their members and provided also that whatever arrangements are made apply only to those who have freely signed up to them. John Sneed remarks that the function of an anarchist as anarchist is not to endorse any particular economic system but 'to destroy the State in order to allow all economic systems to compete on a voluntary basis'[14] and I would accept this point, merely extending it to include any set of voluntary arrangements that do not violate the non-aggression principle.

The caricature of the anarchist as the bomb-throwing bearded Russian leftist is not without some (remote) foundation in fact. I think it fair to say that the common public understanding of anarchism is that it is predominantly if not exclusively a left-wing doctrine and one associated with those inclined to engage in what is sometimes euphemistically referred to as direct action. No surprise then that the English Riots of August 2011 were repeatedly referred to by the reporting news media as being instances of anarchy.

All forms of anarchism have in common their rejection of the state but differ from one another primarily in respect of the position they adopt towards the implications of liberty and, in particular, in their attitude towards the nature, role and legitimacy of property in human society. All forms of leftwing anarchism – anarcho-communism, anarcho-collectivism, syndicalism and mutualism – are unanimous in their rejection of the coercive state but also, to different degrees, either suspicious or completely dismissive of the idea of the private ownership of natural resources, considering such ownership to be restrictive of human liberty. A suspicion of the validity of the private ownership of natural resources would seem to lie at the root of the left-libertarian position that we find in the work of Peter Vallentyne, Michael Otsuka and others.[15] For left libertarians of the Vallentyne-Otsuka persuasion, natural resources belong to everyone in some a priori egalitarian manner so that robust ownership of them (such as ownership without positive obligations to others) by individuals cannot be justified. For the left-libertarians, this rejection of the robust ownership of natural resources requires their owners to pay a rent or tax *as a matter of justice* to those without access to those resources. This rent or tax would have to be paid to and distributed by some agency (if not, how else would it be done?) that, for these purposes at least, would constitute a de facto state inasmuch as it would have to have the power to compel its payment. Insofar as there appears to be an argument for the left-anarchist and left-libertarian approach to the ownership of natural resources, it seems to depend on the claim that since they are not created by any human being we have no reason to believe that their original appropriators are entitled to all their benefits. In contrast, libertarian anarchism regards the robust ownership of natural resources as an intrinsic element in human liberty. Natural resources – property – is the dividing issue between libertarian anarchists and other libertarians and anarchists. Let us take a closer look at the issue.

Property

In daily speech, property is taken to be things such as cars and bicycles, houses and TV sets – robust physical entities of various kinds. To talk like this is to mistake the material for the formal. Property is not so much a bunch of things such as cars or TVs but rather a set of rights to dispose, completely or partially, of such things in a variety of ways.

Possession is a factual matter that can, for the most part, be determined by observation and any living thing can possess other things. Ownership, on the other hand, is a normative notion and implies the right to dispose of things, even things that one does not currently possess. You can own things and not possess them; possess them and not own them. I can own a house that is currently occupied or possessed by someone else, say, my tenant. My ownership of the house gives me the ultimate right to dispose of it even if I am temporarily restricted in the exercise of that right. Only beings that have the capacity to grasp the idea of ownership, that is, only rational beings, can own things.

Any kind of thing that can be sufficiently demarcated can be the object of ownership. The possibility of demarcation is largely a technological matter. At one time, radio frequencies were not sufficiently demarcatable to be able to be the objects of ownership; now they are. You can own inanimate objects, such as natural resources (apples, fields) and manufactured objects (pens, laptops, wheelbarrows and houses.) You can own animate objects such as cats, dogs and donkeys. In the case of animals, we are not concerned with their possibly rich if completely unknowable internal life, their cognitive abilities or their desires. To own a donkey, you do not have to know or be concerned with or be able to control its knowledge or its feelings, you just have to have the right to dispose of its services.

E. Adamson Hoebel takes a conventionalist approach to the concept of property, arguing that possessions only become property when recognized as such by society at large. Things do not become property 'until the members of the society at large agree, tacitly or explicitly, to bestow the property attribute upon the object by regulating their behavior with respect to it in a self-limiting respect'.[16] On the other hand, Anthony de Jasay energetically disputes the idea that property is socially produced, which idea, he thinks, would imply that individual owners hold their property only by the grace and favour of the rest of society: 'Property is not necessarily a social product. It can come about by individual effort totally isolated from society. . . .'[17]

It would seem that these positions cannot both be true at the same time and in the same respect, yet there is something intuitively plausible about both of them. Hoebel's conventionalist approach recognizes that rights are jural matters and are therefore embedded in a human social context. Ownership is not something that can be seen, heard or touched. It is a trilateral relationship among persons in relation to an object. In contrast, and I think incorrectly, Anthony de Jasay defines ownership as a bilateral 'relation between an owner and the thing owned, such that the owner is at liberty to use it, to concede specific rights in it to others, and to alienate it, as well as to exclude access to it by others except with his consent'.[18] Defined trilaterally, property has two aspects: the object owned, and the network of social relationships that establish the normative or jural connection between persons and the object. On the other hand – and here, I think, de Jasay is correct – property rights are not, at least not initially, arbitrary social creations but in some sense a recognition by the members of a society of the validity of a pre-existing claim by one or more of its members in respect of some object or other.

Consider the following.[19] There are two opposing positions in respect of the ownership of natural resources; we can hold that such resources are initially owned by mankind in common or we can hold that they are initially unowned. If natural resources are initially unowned then while they may well be *acquired* by Andrew they cannot, as a matter of logic, be acquired *unjustly*.[20] For injustice to enter into the transaction, the acquisition of the resources would have to involve some transgression against some other person, let us say, Barbara. What could this transgression possibly be if not the violation of Barbara's right to those resources which implies that Barbara must have owned those resources before Andrew acquired them from her. The upshot of all this is that if the acquisition is to be unjust it cannot be initial – the resources must already be owned. For any acquisition to be initial the resources acquired have to be unowned.

But what if the natural resources were initially owned in common? Would it not now be the case that any acquisition or attempted acquisition by a particular person or particular group of people would constitute a violation of the rights of all others not consensually involved in the transaction and so be unjust? Once again, however, we have a problem. If natural resources are initially owned by everyone then while an attempt by Andrew to acquire some of those resources for himself might conceivably be unjust it could not be an injustice in initial acquisition. At most it could be an injustice in transfer.

This brings us back to the two opposing positions with respect to the ownership of natural resources. The two basic options mentioned above – natural resources are initially owned by mankind in common or natural resources are initially unowned – are often taken to be equally tenable. A moment's reflection will show that this is not so. Imagine a world without human beings. Who owns it? Leaving theological reflections to one side, the answer has to be 'no one' simply because there *is* in fact no one to own anything. Now let us admit Adam and Eve onto the scene, living happily, for the moment, in the Garden of Eden. Do they own the whole world, including those parts of it that they have never seen, visited or used such as Alaska or deepest Siberia? If you are inclined to answer yes to this question, ask yourself if, by parity of reasoning, they could also be said to own Pluto or Betelgeuse, entities of whose existence they are similarly not aware. Now substitute for Adam and Eve all the human beings in existence in, say, 35000 BC, living somewhere in East Africa. Suppose they number 500,000. Do *they* own the whole world – Alaska and Siberia included – collectively? Claims of ownership cannot be constituted by mere existence. In order to acquire property, one must *do* something specific (mould, fence, clear) *to* something specific (this piece of clay, this piece of open ground, this section of woodland) with the intention (which can be latent) to exclude others from its use.[21]

If common ownership were taken to be not collective but distributive so that everyone owned some particular proportionate portion of the world, we still encounter insuperable problems. Which portions do we get? And of what? Land, minerals, animals, fish, radio frequencies? And how is our apportionment affected by the inevitable arrival of newcomers? Will we need to constantly re-divide the resources to accommodate our growing population? G. A. Cohen accused Robert Nozick of being 'blithe' in assuming that natural resources are initially unowned[22] but it is rather those who assume common ownership who are blithe and who must stand convicted of defending an incoherent and untenable position.

Although the inadequacies of the Lockean metaphor of mixing one's labour with external resources as a criterion of their ownership have often been pointed out,[23] there nonetheless remains something intuitively attractive about it. If I pick up a piece of driftwood and carve it into a statue of the Infant Samuel at prayer, it is difficult to see how the resultant statue could be considered anyone's but mine. The core of the Lockean metaphor is that one must *do* something to acquire natural resources – one acquires nothing by sitting around and looking pretty – and that something must have the effect of altering them or controlling them or demarcating them in some significant way so as to exclude others from using them. Exclusion is, I believe, the key element in the notion of initial acquisition. It is not enough merely to be first; one has to be first *in acquiring* and acquiring means appropriating resources in such a way as to exclude their use by others. How this exclusion is to be manifested depends on the nature of the resources appropriated.

Something of this notion of exclusion remains in the common law doctrine of adverse possession. If someone without legal title to a piece of land treats it in such a way as to assert ownership of it (say, for example, by building on it or fencing it off from surrounding land) and if the holder of the title takes no action to assert his rights to the land, then the adverse possessor will, after a certain time, be able to assert a title superior to that of the original holder. The failure of the original title holder to exclude the adverse possessor is taken to be tantamount to an abandonment of his claim to title.

Now, suppose that, living alone on a desert island, you were to clear some ground, plant some carrots and give them the tender loving care that they need until they were ready to be picked and eaten. Would you not own the carrots? I would rather say that if you were to live in such radical social isolation, you would neither own nor not own the carrots: the question of ownership simply would not arise. But now, suppose another person were to appear and attempt to appropriate the carrots, what then? In that case, you would be in a position to make a counterclaim that, all things considered, would seem to be better grounded than that of the challenger. In so doing, you would be attempting to actualize a kind of latent or virtual ownership that pre-existed any actual claim or recognition of that claim by others.

It would seem that in the course of human history, after the first agricultural revolution, when people began to cultivate crops and domesticate animals, work was required to bring land under cultivation or to make it suitable for pasture. This work represented an expenditure of labour that could not easily be recovered if the one who expended it could legitimately be forced to give it up by others. At this stage, however, we still have de facto possession rather than ownership or, if ownership, then only virtual or latent ownership. That virtuality became actualized when other land users settled around the original user and, requiring undisturbed possession of their own tracts, were able to demand this only if there was mutual recognition not just of the fact of possession but of the right so to possess; in a word, a recognition of property.

These reciprocal claims, of course, require that the boundaries between adjacent properties be reasonably clearly demarcated, a requirement celebrated in the proverb that 'Good fences make good neighbours.'[24] 'As people began to lay claims to territory and to mark by signs what they regarded as their territory, neighbors started, in some cases at least, to accommodate themselves to these claims. To do this, though, it had to be true that neighbors could discern and were prepared to respect the boundaries of territorial claims.'[25]

Acquisition is a kind of virtual ownership that becomes actual ownership by means of reciprocal recognition. In this way, Hoebel's and de Jasay's approaches can be reconciled. My settled use and reuse of my possessions requires you to refrain from interfering with them, but your use and reuse of your possessions also requires me to refrain from interfering with them. Mutual recognition of one another's exclusive control amounts to the transformation of factual possession into normative ownership. Cicero wrote that private property has been endowed.

> not by nature, but by longstanding occupancy in the case of those who settled long ago on empty land; or by victory in the case of those who gained it in that way; or by law or bargain or contract or lot. . . . since what was by nature common property has passed into the ownership of individuals, each should retain what has accrued to him, and if anyone seeks any of it for himself, he will transgress the law of the community.[26]

The requirement of reciprocal recognition cannot sensibly be made a spatio-temporal universal requirement but must be limited to one's immediate neighbours in space and time. Recognition of your property claims by those geographically remote is not required; still less is it the case that your property claims demand the recognition of those yet to be born.

The libertarian theorists Linda and Morris Tannehill who are sceptical of the Lockean labour-mixing metaphor as a criterion of resource acquisition, question the objectionability of the 'first come' principle: 'If the first comers were ambitious, quick and intelligent enough to acquire the property before anyone else, why should they be prevented from reaping the rewards of these virtues in order to hold the land open for someone else?' Primary acquisition does not exclude others for all time for it is not enough to have the luck and skill to acquire property, one must also have the luck and skill to hold onto it. 'And if a large chunk of land is acquired by a man who is too stupid or lazy to make a productive use of it, other men, operating within the framework of the free market, will eventually be able to bid it away from him and put it to work producing wealth.'[27] Anthony de Jasay is in sympathy with David Hume who regarded initial exclusion as a simple matter of fact. For Hume, he writes, 'initial exclusion is a matter of fact; it happens by "first occupation." At that point, society is formed by the "first assignment" to the "present possessor." The morality of these steps is not at issue'.[28]

Some preliminary criticisms of anarchy

Here are some commonly expressed objections to the idea that a society could function under anarchy. Some of these points, especially the ones relating to law, order and justice, are treated more substantially in other chapters of the book. Many objections to anarchy concern themselves with anarchy's alleged inability to supply things such as roads, water, garbage disposal services and the like. Whatever the merits of such objections, I am not concerned with them here. As John Hasnas has argued, the fundamental argument for anarchy must show only that a central authority is not necessary for the provision of any *essential* service.[29] Such essential services he believes to be, as I do, law, justice and policing.

> *Anarchy is committed to an abstract individualism that makes it impossible for it to give a coherent account of human co-operation and community.*[30]

There may be some anarchists who subscribe to such abstract individualism but libertarian anarchists have no principled commitment to it. John Hoffman, who makes this criticism, would appear to have thinkers such as William Godwin or Max Stirner in mind. According to Hoffman, Godwin's radical individualism is such that 'co-operation, organization and even direct democracy all infringe personal autonomy'.[31] That may be true for Godwin and even, perhaps, for Stirner, both of whom appear to Hoffman as quasi-Hobbesians who see the human world as an arena for the conduct of a war involving all against all. For both of these thinkers it would appear that anything such as goals, purposes and ends 'are oppressive even if they are imposed by individuals upon themselves'.[32] I have made it clear that in my account of libertarian anarchism, human beings are free to form whatever groups or organizations they choose. As long as their commitments to these organizations are voluntary, there can be no question of coercion or aggression. However pertinent Hoffman's criticism might be for some particular forms of anarchism, it completely misses the mark if the target is libertarian anarchism.

> *Those who advocate libertarian anarchism are unable to solve the problems of social division and inequality.*[33]

The problems of social division and inequality may well be insoluble by any political system. If that is so, then the failure of libertarian anarchism to solve these problems counts no more against it than against any other system. Hoffman's judgement on this matter cannot be empirical (it is hard to know how one would establish this empirically) but must be a priori. Libertarian anarchism contends that much, if not most, of the poverty, inequality and social division that characterizes human society is a product of systemic aberrations introduced and maintained by the state. There are reasons for thinking that the state provision of any good or service is always more expensive and less efficient than that produced by the free market. If so, these expensive inefficiencies would appear in the state's financing and supply of social goods just as much as in any other. The evidence for the libertarian case is partly empirical but mostly a priori. Whatever the outcome of relevant comparisons, as an attack on libertarian anarchism this criticism fails to grip.

> *Anarchist societies of the past employed social and moral controls that were no less coercive than any putative state coercion of the present day.*

It is true that traditional societies tended to extend the reach of the law beyond the realm of strict justice and into the areas of moral and social control. Additionally, in such societies individuals tended to be subordinated to their kinship groups. It does not follow from this, however, that this is a necessary feature of anarchist societies as such any more than monarchy, once a staple of all polities, is a necessary feature of the state.

> *Anarchists cannot get rid of the state without resorting to state-like measures to do so.*[34]

How do we get from state-centred society to a stateless one? This question, Hoffman thinks, is unanswerable. Those who put this objection forward appear to believe this is a problem for anarchists because anarchists by definition have to oppose any form of organization. But while this may be true for some anarchists, it is certainly not true for all. In the libertarian anarchy I espouse, the libertarian part of it is what permits people voluntarily to join together in any way they choose. And one of those ways could be the setting up of organizations or groups dedicated to the non-violent disestablishment of the state, just as some state Churches (such as the Church of Ireland, for example) were disestablished in the past.

> *Anarchy will not work because it is fundamentally unstable. Human beings desire power and someone always tries to grab it. Nothing is going to change that.*

The existence of the state offers a prize that those who are hungry for power can contend for. Not all human violence has its origin in the state but wars, the most extreme and extensive form of inter-human violence, are fought either between states or within states as one group or another attempts to seize hold of the reins of state power. The existence of states only facilitates some of those few people with antisocial desires who want to dominate others. A deeper problem with this criticism is that it poisons the wells. If all human beings are intrinsically power-hungry and savage, how can we solve our problems by giving ultimate law-making and law-enforcing authority to one particular group of such appalling animals? There is a fundamental problem with the 'we need the state' argument if it is based on a conception of human beings as essentially diabolical. Those who are to operate the levers of state power must be drawn from those very same demonic people whose need to be restrained led us to create the state in the first place. Who will restrain those to whom we have given all the power and all the weapons? And if *they* do not need to be so restrained, why do the rest of us need to be? As Sartwell puts it: '. . . to cure people of the selfishness and violence at our hearts, we will heavily arm some of them and authorize them to restrain, imprison, or execute others of them'.[35] Hmmm. Yes. Sounds like a good idea.

> *You could not have any form of governance under anarchy as anarchy requires that everyone agree with every decision and once a society reaches a certain critical mass, unanimity is impossible.*

Chapter 5 is devoted to showing that law emerges covalently with any and every society. In the meantime, we can say that the application of the non-aggression principle and its instantiation in rules of conduct will provide the basic laws that any society needs to protect life, limb and property. Positive laws would be created by agreement within voluntary groups of varying sizes by the methods they themselves determine. Those unhappy with the positive regulations of a voluntary group to which they belong can withdraw from them and join another.

> *Anarchy would not stop people from breaking the law.*

True. No system can entirely prevent those absolutely determined to do wrong from doing it. The libertarian anarchist contention is not that under anarchy things would be perfect but that they would be better than they now are. The number of activities deemed to be criminal would be severely reduced and confined to those that violated the principle of non-aggression. The prisons, if there were any, would be emptied of those now imprisoned because they have committed victimless crimes.

Anarchy can only work if people cooperate. It could not be imposed involuntarily.

Yes, anarchy cannot be imposed if, as seems likely, that imposition required the initiatory use of force or violence. Anarchy requires cooperation essentially only in the avoidance of aggression and history shows that most people will cooperate in this, even if only for reasons of self-interest and mutual benefit. Chapter 5 is devoted to showing that law can emerge and be maintained in the absence of a coercive state.

Just as people now insure themselves against catastrophic risk, in anarchy, people would contract with others to defend them against aggression. Agencies would develop devoted to the provision of protection and the securing of justice. Competing defence and justice agencies would inevitably engage in conflict with one another or coalesce into a super defence agency that would, in effect, be a state.

This is essentially Robert Nozick's argument in *Anarchy, State, and Utopia*. There is every market incentive for different agencies *not* to compete aggressively with one another and to work out in advance of any actual disputes how those would be resolved. There is no more a necessary momentum towards one super-agency than there is towards any other natural monopoly. The same economic and social dynamics apply here as elsewhere. If the super-agency that arose through natural monopoly supplied its services well and at a reasonable rate, competitors would be kept out by market forces. If the super-agency started to provide a poor service or to increase its charges significantly then competitors would enter the field and, unless driven from it by force (for example, by a proto-state), would provide the necessary competition to keep the quality of services up and prices down. There is no reason to think that the provision of defence and justice is a natural monopoly.

If we look at countries that now have no government and compare them with well-governed liberal states, who would want to live in the former rather than the latter?

There is an old rule of thumb in the human sciences that in statistical comparisons between two sets of phenomena the best of the worst is always better than the worst of the best. Take a non-contentious example. It seems obvious that men are taller than women. If someone were to try to counter this claim by pointing out that Matilda, at six foot four, is considerably taller than Percy, at five foot two, this would not make the original claim false. To say that 'Men are taller than women' is *not* to imply that every man is taller than any woman; it is simply to compare average measurements in the two classes of entities, one against another. Similarly, it is not particularly insightful to compare a radically underdeveloped society X in a state of quasi-anarchy with a society Z that is governed by a state but which has benefitted from three or four hundred years of relative socioeconomic freedom. A maximally flourishing society requires the elimination of the state but also a lot more; anarchy is only a necessary but not a sufficient condition for such a society. Later, we will take a look at some quasi-anarchistic societies. The point of such an examination is not to suggest that these societies were or are desirable places to live, it is simply to show that societies based on anarchic principles are possible and to extract from an examination of them some principles upon which a contemporary anarchic society could be constructed, shorn of their historically conditioned limitations.

If the state did not create law, we would all live in a neo-Hobbesian condition of constant mutual predation.

The response to this objection is the substance of Chapter 5. In the meantime, it might be worthwhile to point out that the bulk of the rules by which we live together from day to day were not in fact created by government which, of course, shows that government is not necessary for their creation. Hasnas makes the point that much of the so-called Common Law is case generated in the context of dispute resolution. Despite what is often thought, it is *not* judge-made, as if judges sat around the Legal and Conservative Club thinking up rules and regulations for people to follow. 'English common law is, in fact, case-generated law; that is, law that spontaneously evolves from the settlement of actual disputes. Almost all of the law that provides the infrastructure of our contemporary society was created in this way' and this includes tort law, property law, contract law, commercial law[36] and even criminal law. While it is certainly the case that an ever increasing amount of our law is encompassed in statutes, 'the fact that politicians recognise the wisdom of the common law by enacting it into statutes, hardly proves that government is necessary to create rules of law. Indeed, it proves precisely the opposite'.[37]

> *Whatever else might be supplied by market forces, surely we could not have private courts. Private courts would be productive of rampant social chaos.*

Considerations relevant to answering this objection are treated in Chapter 5. In the meantime, suffice it to say that much of the difficulty in accepting as viable the libertarian proposals in this area arise from a simple failure of historical imagination. Because things are the way they are, we tend to presume that this is how they always have been and always must be. So, because we have a state-supported monopolistic court system, we tend to assume that this is how things have always been and how they have to be. But a glance at our history will dispel the notion that things have always been this way. Europe has had multiple and overlapping legal jurisdictions for most of its history[38] and it is really only since the emergence of the modern state in the seventeenth century that we have had the development, under state control, of the judicial systems with which we are now acquainted. Even in contemporary western societies, we have de facto multiple legal jurisdictions. John Hasnas gives the following examples: the London Commercial Court,

JAMS/Endispute, the American Arbitration Association and so on. As a matter of fact, we do not have uniformity of laws throughout the world; laws vary from one country to another. Even within some countries, we have multiple legal systems as in Britain, for example, where England and Wales have one legal system and Scotland another and in the USA where each state has its own set of laws. Despite this plurality of multiple jurisdictions, there is a convergence towards a common set of basic laws so that all jurisdictions have rules, very similar rules, on the prohibition of murder, manslaughter, assault, battery, theft and extortion. A glance around the world at the moral codes of different traditions will show an astonishing convergence; astonishing, at least, if one has not yet grasped that without such rules, no society can exist. Of course, the scope, extent and precise delimitation of these rules vary from one place to another but the rules are essentially the same. In things that are not nearly so significant, there can be diversity and there is. But why should this be a problem?[39] Roderick Long argues that variety has been the spice of legal life for systems of law. The market produces uniformity when uniformity is needed and diversity when diversity is needed. It is not a simple matter of having either total uniformity or total diversity. As analogies, he instances the shape of the standard credit card and the videotape convergence on the VHS standard; these show a dynamic tendency towards uniformity while, on the other hand, the bewildering variety of goods and services – different films, many types of bread, lots of different makes of car – show a dynamic tendency towards increasing diversity. In legal matters, the relatively uniform law merchant of the Middle Ages emerged when the variety of local legal systems failed to provide a stable legal environment for international trade.

Without government, we will not have unbiased judges[40]

We can agree that we need impartial arbiters if justice is to be done but why does that imply the necessity for a monopoly government? The argument appears to be if each person should delegate arbitration to an impartial third party arbitrator then there has to be one and only one third party that fulfils that role. Roderick Long rightly sees that there is a logical fallacy here involving an illicit quantifier shift. If we assume we are talking only about people and take 'D' to stand for the two place predicate – '[blank] should delegate powers of arbitration to [blank]' – then in logical terms the argument runs: $(x)(Ey)Dxy \rightarrow (Ey)(x)Dxy$. In English, this reads: if it is the case that for everyone there is some person or other to whom they should all delegate arbitration, then it follows that there is one specific person to whom everybody should delegate arbitration. This is a bit like saying that if everyone owns a pair of shoes, there is some one pair of shoes that everyone owns which, of course, is nonsense.

We need a state to produce and enforce regulations controlling the activities of some individuals.

Every functioning society has to have regulations to control the amount of intentional or reckless harm that one person may inflict on another. Some regulatory systems such as ethics and religious regulations are informal; some such as law are formal. Tort law is the normal form that such formal regulation takes and tort law is not in origin a state product. As Hasnas says, 'There may be many things wrong with contemporary tort law, but being ineffective at internalising externalities is most assuredly not among them. The only way to believe that government is necessary to resolve the problem of social costs is to be studiously blind to the nature of both common law and government legislation.'[41]

But surely we would have to have a unified police force to maintain law and order?

Once again, what gives rise to this objection is either a failure of imagination or a failure of collective memory. People simply forget (or never knew in the first place) that people provided policing services privately for themselves as they needed them without government assistance. Societies have existed for aeons before ever there was a perceived need for a state-sponsored police force. Non-political methods of enforcing order are endemic in any functioning society; without them, no society could function. We did not get the first government-sponsored police force in Britain until the creation of the Bow Street Runners and even they were semi-private. The British Bobby, prototype for all other state police forces, did not come into being until early in the nineteenth century.

It is not insignificant that the new police forces were modelled on the Police Preservation Force (PPF) established by Sir Robert Peel in 1814 in Ireland (afterwards called the Royal Irish Constabulary (RIC), 1836) that operated as a paramilitary force, being recruited largely from ex-soldiers and consisting of some 8,000–10,000 men housed in 1,400 barracks across the country. When transplanted to Britain, the new police forces modelled on the PPF (RIC) were not uniformly welcomed. In complaints that eerily echo complaints that are still made today 'Ratepayers objected to having to pay for a body of men that, unlike the old watchmen, were not under their control. Those in the wealthier parishes complained that there were now fewer men patrolling their streets than there had been when they ran their own watches. The poor objected to the ways in which the new constables interfered with their behaviour on the streets.'[42]

There were those who suspected that the new force would be used as an instrument of political repression. One newspaper of the day, the *Weekly Dispatch*, described the new Bobbies as 'a military force employed in civil duties' and was of the opinion that 'it is a powerful engine in the hands of Government' that 'may be employed for the suppression of public freedom'.[43] Today, just as in their beginning, state police forces are used not just to prosecute offences against justice but to enforce a whole range of paternalistic policies such as discouraging smoking, enforcing the wearing of seatbelts and much else that the state considers socially desirable. No private police force would bother with such things – the cost is too high and the nuisance (such as it is) too small and, in any event, none of these things is an offence against justice.

If the policeman's lot is not a happy one, the lot of those undergoing the policing has not been significantly happier. Emsley notes that the purpose of policing has shifted inexorably from being an instrument of community defence 'to becoming an instrument of the state with, at the beginning of the twenty-first century, targets set and regulated centrally for the good of what politicians and policing professionals consider as the national community'.[44]

Where the only forms of policing are those provided by the state, where the natural self-policing of society by itself has been legally discouraged, we have effective chaos and the reversion of sections of the population to an almost feral state. John Hasnas remarks that 'Arguing that the high rate of inner-city crime and the presence of gangs implies that we must maintain a government monopoly on police services is a bit like arguing that the abysmal quality of inner-city public schools implies that we should not permit parents to use their tax money to send their children to private schools.'[45] In the English riots of 2011, the police largely just stood by while looters ransacked and burned shops; shop owners who attempted to defend their property against attack were treated as if *they* were the law-breakers.

Emancipate yourself from the imaginative tyranny of the present and ask yourself how you would go about creating an institution responsible for securing people's lives, limbs and property. Would you select a small group of people who like ordering other people around, give them all the weapons, take all the weapons from everybody else, make everyone in society pay them no matter how effective or ineffective they were in doing what they were supposed to do and have them answerable to the extent that they are answerable, not to you and your fellow members of society but to some other group of individuals who may or, more likely, may not have the same agenda that you do? Or would you do something else?

5
LAW WITHOUT ORDERS

In the darkest days of World War I, the following conversation took place in the trenches between the cowardly and cynical Captain Blackadder and the foolish but phlegmatic Private Baldrick. Baldrick is puzzled about something which, given his generally dismal level of intelligence, is hardly surprising. He puts his problem squarely in front of Captain Blackadder: '. . . these days there's a war on, right? And, ages ago, there wasn't a war on, right? So, there must have been a moment when there not being a war on went away, right, and there being a war on came along.' Blackadder is wondering where this rambling rumination is going and how much longer it is going to take. Baldrick continues: 'So, what I want to know is: How did we get from the one case of affairs to the other case of affairs?' Astonished at Baldrick's apparently entertaining a coherent if badly expressed thought, Blackadder asks him, just to make sure: 'Do you mean "How did the war start?"' and Baldrick, gratified to have his meaning grasped so readily, responds: 'Yeah.'[1] To paraphrase Baldrick, these days we have a myriad of laws (in the words of Lord Philips of Sudbury 'The whole thing is farcical, it's a tsunami. We're drowning in the stuff'[2]) and ages ago we did not. So it would seem that there must have been a moment when there not being laws went away and there being laws came along. How did we get from one case of affairs to the other? How did law start?

Where does law come from? [3]

At the stage at which it enters our historical consciousness, law is already the product of a long period of social evolution. It is possible to define law in such a way that its origin becomes relatively recent. J. H. Baker does just this in his *An Introduction to English Legal History* in which law is defined as 'a body of known and uniform rules, enforced by the state through its courts'.[4] If you believe, as I do, that the state that we have come to know and love is an entity that came into being for the most part in the seventeenth century, that would make law a relative recent invention, a claim that is somewhat implausible. Even if one were to lift one's historical gaze so that it rested on the Code of Hammurabi and concluded from this that state-sponsored law goes back at least four thousand years or so, that would still make law a relatively recent phenomenon in the context of the whole of human existence. Rather than having any essential connection to the state, ancient or modern, it is much more likely – indeed, how could it *not* be the case – that law, in the sense of fundamental regulative norms, is constitutive of every functioning human society. Try to imagine what it would be like to have a society, any kind of society, without enforceable regulative norms. It is true that these laws are not likely to have been made by a specialist body of legislators nor will they be published in an official gazette; nonetheless, they are recognizably laws and perhaps even the most fundamental kind of laws we can have.

This socially constitutive law is therefore coeval with society and must be antecedent to the more variable, mutable and idiosyncratic elements of culture. Without common rules, human beings could not live together in peace and society would be impossible. That being so, as Hayek notes, it would have to be the case that 'Long before man had developed language to the point where it enabled him to issue general commands, an individual would be accepted as a member of a group only so long as he conformed to its rules.'[5] Whatever connection such fundamental law has with the modern state, then, is historically contingent.

The conditions for the emergence of law

The biological and psychosocial evolutionary processes that allowed our pre-human ancestors to transmute themselves into homo sapiens are necessarily shrouded in the mists of history. We have no written or oral accounts of this prehistoric period unless we assume, and it would be just an assumption, that the earliest myths of which we have record contain some historical nuggets. Whether or not this is so, any account of what happened during this long period of time is bound to be speculative. Despite this, it should still be possible to sketch in rough outline the conditions for the emergence of law. Here, in brief, is what is required. In order to have law, we need a plurality of embodied rational beings, minimally three, existing in proximate relation to each another, in the context of scarce resources. Let us discuss them in order of embodiment, scarcity, rationality, relatedness and plurality.

Embodiment

There may or may not be purely spiritual beings, such as the angels of Zoroastrian, Jewish and Christian tradition. If there are any such, it may be that they can come into conflict with one another in some way. However that may be, on the basis of reason alone there is little that we can know for certain about such beings, let alone their modes of social or asocial interaction.[6] In contrast to these immaterial beings, human beings are essentially and demonstrably embodied and the first and inalienable property that each person has is in his own body. As embodied beings, we take up space. While we do not have to be anywhere in particular, we have to be somewhere. We are not only spatial beings; we are also essentially temporal. Our existence unrolls over time and since we are mortal, time is, for each of us, *the* ultimate non-renewable resource. Our relations with other human beings are essentially mediated through our spatio-temporal bodies and that gives rise to the possibility not only of cooperation but also of competition.

Scarcity

If our bodies are our first and most fundamental properties, they are far from being our only property. Being embodied, we of necessity have to stake a claim to the use of a portion of the earth's resources and that eventually requires the development of the notion of property in external objects. If we lived in a magical world in which we could have anything we wanted simply by desiring it then it is difficult to see how the concept of external property could develop at all. Let us imagine that I have a Rolls Royce. It is the only one actually in existence. You want one too so, in the normal course of events, you would either have to persuade me to sell you mine, build one for yourself or have someone else build one for you, all at the appropriate cost. As it happens, you are a magician so you do not need to persuade me to sell you mine or have someone make one for you; all you have to do is to wave your wand, utter the magic words and conjure another Rolls Royce out of thin air. In a magical world, you could have possessions but since scarcity has no meaning in such a world, the notion of property in external objects would have no purchase and, without property, the need for law is seriously reduced. (It would not be eliminated entirely since, even in this world, one would have a property in oneself.) Property arises in conditions of scarcity which, for our purposes, means not some absolute sub-optimal quantity of goods or services but the situation in which two or more human beings require the use or possession of one good or service in physically incompatible ways.

Rationality

A non-rational animal, let us say a dog, can possess a bone or a bear can dispute the occupation of a cave with another bear, but no sense could be given to a dog or a bear's having the concept of ownership. Ownership is a normative concept – it is not just possession but rightful or lawful possession. While two dogs may squabble over the possession of a bone it makes no sense to say that the victorious canine *owns* the bone. As Adam Smith noted in *The Wealth of Nations* 'Nobody ever saw a dog make a fair and deliberate exchange of one bone for another with another dog. Nobody ever saw one animal by its gestures and natural cries signify to another, this is mine, that yours. . . .'[7]

Relatedness and plurality

Why, for the emergence of law, must our embodied beings exist in relation to each other, and why do we need a minimum of three? Imagine Andrew alone on an island. What possible point could law have in this context? After all, 'human law is framed for a number of human beings, the majority of whom are not perfect in virtue'.[8] Andrew is an embodied rational being and the resources of the island including those of his own bodily being and its temporal conditions are scarce, but what would be the point of law given that there are no social relations to regulate. Andrew could, if he found time hang heavy on his hands, work out an elaborate law code, but since this code could have no possible application its elaboration would be as pointless as playing chess against himself. Of course, Andrew is free to set standards against which he measures his own conduct but these first-person norms can be said to be law only in the most attenuated of senses. This is the realm of personal ethics.[9]

Now, let Barbara wash up on the island. Suppose she lands on a side of the island that is separated from Andrew's domain by an impassable mountain range. To all intents and purposes Andrew is still alone. Eliminate the mountain range and put Andrew and Barbara in contact with each other. Surely now we have the appropriate material circumstances in which law can arise? Again, however, the answer is no. When only two people exist in relation to each other, there can be no law, only agreement or disagreement, because where only two people are present another essential element of law, the neutral resolution of disputes, is not possible. For this we need a third party. If an agreement between the two parties is not achievable and, as is the case on this hypothesis, no independent determination of the merits of the case is possible, the only remedy is self-help by one or other or both of the parties.

The context for the emergence of law

Imagine a dispute to arise. It doesn't matter for our purposes whether the dispute arises as a result of deliberate malice, negligence or mistake. Such a dispute can be resolved in three possible ways: by agreement, by violence or by adjudication. Agreement and adjudication are peaceful methods of dispute resolution; violence manifestly is not. Agreement is sometimes, perhaps quite often, possible. Many disputes are avoided or resolved by the willingness of the parties to compromise or by the willingness of one or other simply to yield. However, agreement is not always possible. What then? When both parties maintain their claims and agreement is not possible the matter can be resolved only by violence or by adjudication.

Violence is expensive and inherently risky. It is expensive in that if a dispute escalates into an open conflict, the increase in overall wealth resulting from the division of labour and comparative advantage will diminish or disappear altogether and that is mutually non-beneficial, and that is not to mention the possibility of collateral damage.[10] As Virgil 'the Turk' Sollozzo says to the Corleone's consigliere, Tom Hagen, in *The Godfather*, 'I don't like bloodshed, I'm a businessman and blood costs too much money.'[11] Violence is inherently risky inasmuch one or other of the disputants could be killed or injured which is why 'One of the first causes of a legal system is the desire to prevent or discourage feuding and private warfare. . . .'[12] Both parties to the dispute (and their neighbours also) therefore have an interest in its peaceful resolution. As Bruce Benson notes, even in primitive societies 'the cost of violence and the benefits of order . . . were enough to induce the establishment of recognized rules of conduct with an emphasis on individual rights and private property . . .'.[13]

If agreement cannot be reached and violence is not an acceptable option then only adjudication remains.[14] But where Andrew and Barbara are in conflict, neither Andrew nor Barbara can, in relation to that conflict, be the adjudicator without violating the basic requirement of impartiality that people cannot be judges in their own cases. Adjudication, then, requires a third party. Enter Charlie onto the scene in communication with both Andrew and Barbara; now, all the conditions are finally in place for the emergence of law.

Let our dispute be resolved and judgement given. The judgement will have the form: 'X (the pig or whatever) belongs to Barbara.' While Barbara might be happy to hear this and be keen to get on with enjoying the company of her pig, Andrew wants to hear the reason for the judgement. Without a reasoned basis, the judgement is, or will appear to be, arbitrary and this while perhaps sufficient to resolve the immediate dispute is not enough to prevent the emergence of similar disputes in the future. If dispute resolution is more efficient than violence, dispute avoidance is yet more efficient than resolution and that cannot be had by bare unreasoned judgements.

Even if a particular judgement is substantially bizarre, it still has to have an appearance of rationality. In the long term, it will not do for Charlie to simply say that the dispute is to be resolved in Barbara's favour and then for him to go off to lunch, satisfied that he has done his duty. He has to say *why* his judgement should be as it is. Only if disputes are resolved by judgements that have the form *decision + reason (rule)* can they provide guidance for future conduct. This was so even in the process of the medieval trial by ordeal which, according to J. H. Baker, 'was calculated to avoid reasoned decision-making'.[15]

John Hasnas instances the Anglo-Saxon *moot* as an example of how adjudication was actually reached in practice. The *moot* was an assembly of the community that tried to find a mutually acceptable solution to a dispute that threatened to spill over into violence if not resolved, thereby inflicting costs not only on the disputants but on their neighbours as well. If the structure of a new dispute resembled those of an earlier dispute sufficiently, then the *moot* would recall its earlier adjudication and render a similar judgement. Adjudicative principles that were successful, that is, that prevented the outbreak of violence, were retained; those that were not successful were abandoned. While the immediate occasion of a *moot*'s adjudication was the resolution of the dispute immediately before it, its convergence on a set of successful solutions had the effect of enabling people to order their affairs so as to avoid the emergence of disputes in the future.[16]

If Charlie's decision goes against Andrew, why can he not just ignore it? He could, but only at a cost. The loser in a dispute can refuse to accept judgement only if prepared to accept a return to violence and while this is possible, the reason violence was rejected initially, namely, its high risk and high cost, still remains valid as a disincentive. It is therefore in the long-term interests of all to accept judgements, even when these go against their short-term interests.[17]

On the other hand, what is to stop Charlie, the arbitrator, from being hopelessly biased? Simply this. Charlie is not a permanent judge but simply one of three people who have to live together on this island. Even if he is deaf to the blandishments of justice, as a possible litigant in future litigation he has an interest in being scrupulously fair since one of those whom he has judged may, in time, act as judge in a case involving him.[18] A principled commitment to seeing that justice is done because one loves justice is eminently commendable but it is important to realize that, in an anarchic context, self-interest is normally sufficient to produce impartiality.

Though educed from and applied to a specific case, rules are inherently general but generality, while necessary, is not in itself sufficient; the rules must also be abstract, impersonal and impartial. The rule can hardly be 'Whenever Andrew and Barbara have a dispute over a pig, the decision is to go in favour of Barbara'; it must be something like: 'whenever a person's pig destroys another's crops, then the pig is forfeit'. Rules, then, are abstract, impersonal and impartial though, of course, when applied they are applied to concrete circumstances and particular individuals. Once elicited from a particular dispute, a rule has a presumptively valid status for future disputes unless it needs to be expanded or restricted as the result of an apprehension of some feature forced upon the notice of subsequent adjudicators by changed circumstances.[19]

If the rule originally elicited is rationally adequate, then it will fit other disputes with similar fact patterns. Human beings require reasonable certainty as to which kinds of acts are legally permissible and which are not and reasonable certainty, in turn, demands consistency. Consistency requires that the adjudicator give the same or similar judgements in similar circumstances; it also requires that those who have benefitted from one judgement accept other judgements, even those made against them, provided they accept the essential similarity of the circumstances. Decisions, then, to have persuasive force, must be generally acceptable and over time, as society develops, there will be a convergence of rational judgements into a set of principles and rules, much as language develops spontaneously in accordance with rules. The difference is that law will have to be at least partially reflectively appropriated by at least some in the community whereas language can quite well be spoken by all without any *reflective* appropriation of its rules.[20]

Logic is the explicit articulation of the rational practices embodied in argumentation. Grammar is the explicit articulation of the linguistic practices embodied in speaking. Ethics is the explicit articulation of the socially cohesive practices already embodied in interpersonal relations. When we learn logic as a discipline, it enables us to reflectively appropriate what it is we do when we reason and allows us to become better at it; what it does not do is to teach us to do something we have never done before. We learn grammar only after we already speak our native language, not before, and ethics is a meaningless enterprise if we have not already grasped its essence in practice before we begin to think about it. Nobody learns to be ethical by taking Aristotle's 30 drachma course. The sense of the dictum that 'ignorance of the law is no defence' is to be found in the fact that no one who lives in a community can be unaware of how the *basic* rules for peaceful coexistence actually function in that community anymore than a native speaker of a language can be unaware of the rules of the language. To know the law in this sense it is not necessary to be able to state it, defend it or justify it anymore than knowing (implicitly) the rules of say English syntax requires a native speaker to be able to state explicitly what those rules are. I can know that 'Boy the deck burning on stood the' is gibberish in English without being able to say why.[21]

A common objection to an anarchic legal order is that it would be inaccessible. Once we are comparing one real system with another and not with some unattainable perfection, this is not a problem. In a modern sophisticated society with a busy legislature, who can be said to know the law? Take a stroll through any half-decent law library and confine your attention only to the volumes containing statutes. Ask yourself – who knows all this? The answer is, of course, nobody. To the extent that accessibility is necessary, the basic legal principles of an anarchic society are eminently accessible. To the extent that principles require practical elaboration in the context of a living society, accessibility is an issue only for those who need to know the law in order to operate well. If I am not engaged in commerce I have little need to know commercial law, but if I am then its basic principles would be readily available to me in an anarchist society.

In fact, if any kind of law is inaccessible it is the law of the state. In societies with a central political authority and busy legislatures, the legislature will either duplicate the law as it would emerge from an anarchic order or it will produce laws that deviate from such order and which, to the extent that they so deviate, are unnecessary and unjustified. Such law, the law that weighs down the bookshelves of most law libraries, is eminently inaccessible. As Hasnas notes, 'Not only is government not necessary to ensure that the rules of law are accessible, it inevitably renders them less so.'[22]

It might be thought that this account of the emergence of a legal system from the context of dispute resolution implies that the legal system is, as it were, designed and planned by those rendering the adjudications. On the contrary, my contention is that in the real world the fundamental cultural institutions of human society – language, law, logic and morals – are all of them the outcome of a spontaneous evolutionary process which is the creation of no one or no group's design but which is nonetheless rational. Law is not, to use Hayek's term, 'constructively' rational – that is, it is not the product of a pre-practical design. Its rationality is, rather, implicit.[23]

Customary law

The picture of law I have just sketched is that of the law emerging from the processes of adjudication as a kind of endogenous growth as distinct from law as exogenously constructed and imposed on a society from the outside.[24] Such law is not a command of a superior authority backed by force or the threat of force; it is, rather, the delimitation of customarily permissible and impermissible actions, adhered to by members of the community because they accept them as right and natural, and enforced by social disapproval and, ultimately, social exclusion. The effect of such customary law is to 'trace out boundary lines of individual action, within which each person might freely move without exciting the opposition of others. Here we find exhibited in its earliest and simplest form the function of law'.[25]

In such customary law, we find law's three essential elements: an adjudicative procedure, a body of rules and a means of enforcement. There is a dialectical relationship between adjudication and rules: rules emerge from adjudication and, in turn, feed into and constrain future adjudications. First come judgements, based on implicit and inchoate principles. Then, over time, there emerges a more refined and a more explicit grasp of the principles which, in turn, feed into the judgements. We start *ex post* (after the facts) and continue *ex ante* (before the facts) but, as Randy Barnett remarks, 'Even a vintage *ex ante* precept, however, had to be devised and imposed *ex post* for the first time in some case.'[26]

The extent of customary law is severely limited – it ranges over only those aspects of human action that infringe or are capable of infringing on what others perceive (and what the community agrees) are their rights. All other matters are outside the scope of the law. It is true that both morality and law are modes of social control and that some issues, such as homicide or theft, may be the subject of both. Still, while the practical boundary between morality and law is somewhat vague and shifting, conceptually the two modes of social control differ sharply from each other in respect of their content and in their modes of procedures. The subject matter of law is justice, which is a matter of giving to others what is their due and requiring the same from them. The subject matter of morality, on the other hand, ranges from relatively trivial matters that border on etiquette to serious matters such as homicide and theft that clearly overlap with the concerns of justice. In morality, the focus is not so much on satisfying the minimal requirements of justice but on performing actions above and beyond its strict requirements. If you are asked at the end of the day by the significant other in your life what good things you did today and you reply 'Well, I didn't kill anyone and I didn't steal anything' do not be surprised if you fail to receive much praise. To be in line for praise you have to do something more than merely to observe the basics of civilized conduct. The modes of procedure by which morals are enforced are persuasion or exhortation, praise or blame and, if the conduct is egregiously offensive, social exclusion. The mode of procedure that the law ultimately has at its back is an implicit threat of force if the competent judgements of those entitled to make such judgements are not complied with. As Bruce Benson notes '. . . any property rights system is ultimately backed by a threat of force or violence'.[27]

We can note some general characteristics of customary law. The first general characteristic of law whose material elements are constrained by a theory of rights is that it is almost uniformly negative. For the most part, it does not consist of injunctions to do this or to do that but, rather, not to do this or to refrain from doing that. It thus concerns itself with matters relating to the peaceful coexistence of those who live in close proximity and tends to be limited rather than expansive in its operation. The second general characteristic of such law is that it is horizontal; it concerns the adjudication of disputes between two parties, neither of whom stands in a hegemonic relation to the other. This is what is meant by equality before the law. Crime is not a matter of offending a state or a superior but of violating the rights of another. In this context, punishment is primarily a matter of attempting, so far as possible, to restore the status quo ante or, where that is not possible (as in cases of homicide), making a mutually acceptable restitution. The third general characteristic of such an endogenously evolved law is that its enforcement is not achieved by a particular social institution but by the community as a whole by means of disapproval or exclusion or, in extreme cases, outlawry.

In systems of archaic or customary law there is no substantive distinction between criminal law and tort law; the legal system is private, customary and evolutionary; and the aim of justice is primarily restorative, with restitution going to the victims rather than to a state. Enforcement operates via a system of sureties and pledges, the chronically recalcitrant being excluded from society and its protections. Archaic law is rational, evolutionary and horizontal; in contrast, the bulk of contemporary legislation is voluntaristic, revolutionary and vertical. Such archaic law, says Harold Berman, was

> in many respects, a very sensible system. The threat of heavy financial burdens upon the wrongdoer and his kin is probably a more effective deterrent of crime than the threat of capital punishment or corporal mutilation . . . and at least equally effective as the modern sanction of imprisonment; and it is surely less expensive for society. Moreover, in terms of retributive justice, not only is the wrongdoer made to suffer, but in addition – in contrast to today's more 'civilized' penology – the victim is thereby made whole.[28]

It may have occurred to the alert reader that the account given so far neglects what, for most of us, is the first thing we think of when we think of the law, namely, the mass of edicts, rules, regulations and prohibitions that emerge in a seemingly never-ending stream from our legislative assemblies. It can hardly have escaped anyone's notice that the most common method of law-making in operation today is the enactment of statutes by legislative bodies such as the British Parliament or the US Houses of Congress. Such is the grip of our current practices upon our imaginations that many people find it difficult even to conceive, even more difficult to believe, that such a state of affairs is historically contingent and, in fact, relatively recent. 'But,' as Rothbard notes, 'this is historically incorrect . . . . most law, but especially the most libertarian parts of the law, emerged not from the State, but out of non-State institutions . . .'. Such institutions have been 'tribal custom, common-law judges and courts, the law merchant in mercantile courts, or admiralty law in tribunals set up by shippers themselves'.[29] In all these institutions, the task of the judge was not to make law but to find it in existing and generally accepted principles and then to apply it to specific cases or to new technological or institutional conditions. The same was true in private Roman law.[30] It is a maxim of common-law jurisprudence that ignorance of the law is no defence. If knowledge of the law equated to knowledge of legislation, most of us would be rendered completely defenceless. Fortunately, substantive norms often replace substantive laws and although 'most people know little private law and are not much bothered by their ignorance. Their experience tells them that the basic rules that govern ordinary affairs are not in the law books anyway'.[31]

The objection could be raised that even if law emerges more or less in the way I have outlined, there would appear to be nothing to prevent there being a multitude of systems of customary law, some perhaps wildly divergent from others, so that intra-legal conflict would become inevitable. To this we may answer that even as things stand, we have multiple legal systems. Each currently constituted state tends to have a system that differs in significant respects from that of other states and some states, such as the United States of America, even have multiple legal jurisdictions. Conflict of laws, then, is a fact of life but despite this, the different jurisdictions manage to arrange their affairs to minimize conflict and to resolve intersystemic problems adequately.

More fundamentally, however, the restriction of law to matters of justice – the prevention and punishment of aggression – will ensure that there will be a tendency of initially divergent legal systems to converge on a set of common principles. Consider the following example. In every society in which pasturage and tillage exist side by side, some way must be found of preventing damage to crops caused by wandering animals. In English common law, the rule emerged that owners of animals have a duty to fence their animals in. In the western states of the United States of America, on the other hand, given the very different material circumstances, not least the enormous financial burden that a 'fencing-in' rule would impose on ranchers, the rule that emerged was that those growing crops and wishing to avoid incidental damage were obliged to fence wandering animals out. The material outcome is the same in both jurisdictions but the allocation of duties and responsibilities differs significantly.

Our imaginations are limited by the tyranny of the present. We tend to believe, unthinkingly, that the way things are is the ways things always have been and always have to be. The legal systems we have – with their sharp distinction of criminal law from the law of tort, with their idea of crime as an offence against the state, with their presumption that there can be only one system of law in a given territory and with their theories of punishment radically disconnected from any notion of restitution – are historically contingent and mutable. A non-hegemonic legal system (better still, a plurality of legal systems) based on the principles of customary law shorn of its irrational particularistic elements could well answer the needs of social order without permitting the paternalistic interference with liberty that is characteristic of contemporary legal systems.

Natural law

Customary law is a particular and local concretization of natural law, having regard to local conditions and circumstances. Of all essentially contested philosophical terms, 'natural law' surely has to be one of the most contested. The use of this term in some philosophical circles is an incitement to philosophical violence![32] The idea of natural law found its classical expression in the philosophy of the Stoics and was strikingly expressed by Cicero:

> Indeed true law is right reason congruent with nature, spread among all people, constant, everlasting; it calls to duty by ordering and deters from deceit [crime or wrongdoing] by forbidding. Nevertheless neither does it order or forbid upright men in vain, nor does it move the wicked by ordering or forbidding. It is not holy to alter this law, nor is it permitted to modify any part of it, nor can it be entirely repealed. In fact we cannot be released from this law by either the Senate or the people. No Sextus Aelius[33] should be sought as expositor or interpreter. There will not be one law at Rome, another at Athens, one now, another later, but one law both everlasting and unchangeable will encompass all nations and for all time. And one God will be in common as though he were a teacher and general of all people. He will be the author, umpire, and provider of this law. He who will not obey it will flee from himself and, defying human nature, by reason of this very fact will suffer the greatest penalties, even if he escapes other things that are thought to be punishments.[34]

Part of the antipathy experienced by some to natural law arises from the mistaken notion that it necessarily has theological implications and is essentially a form of a 'Divine Command' ethical theory. This is not so and that it is not so has been obvious since the time of Hugo Grotius. Frank van Dun expressed the view that the term 'natural' in 'natural law' is to be taken literally, holding that natural law 'refers to the natural, physical world of living human beings'.[35] Likewise, the 'law' in 'natural law' is not to be understood as a kind of super-statute, a kind of command or directive of some celestial or transcendental lawgiver. It is, instead, to be taken as referring to 'the order or bond of conviviality that has its natural foundation in the plurality and diversity of distinct and separate persons'.[36] Similarly, the renowned legal theorist Lon Fuller who deals in his work with what he takes to be the natural laws of human undertakings clearly states that:

> These natural laws have nothing to do with any 'brooding omnipresence in the skies. . . . They remain entirely terrestrial in origin and application.' These natural laws are not residents of some Empyrean region that descend on us from on high. 'They are not "higher" laws; if any metaphor of elevation is appropriate they should be called "lower" laws. They are like the . . . laws respected by a carpenter who wants the house he builds to remain standing and serve the purpose of those who live in it.'[37]

This naturalistic conception of natural law must be taken seriously. If it is then whatever other objections may be made to it at least some of the more egregious ones will have been antecedently rebutted.

On core issues, and understood formally, all customary legal systems tend to converge on the prohibition of acts sometimes called *mala in se* – acts that are wrong in and of themselves everywhere and always. Thus there is no functioning human society that permits the indiscriminate killing of one of its members by another. A given society may have a severely limited conception of who is to count as one of its members but that is a material, not a formal, matter. Similarly, no society permits the indiscriminate appropriation of the property of one of its members by another. Again, a given society may have an historically conditioned notion of what counts as property but every society must have *some* conception of property or other and whatever that may be it must be generally respected. It should come as no surprise, then, to find that all societies prohibit homicide, assault and theft and require the making good of damage done to persons or property even where the acts causing the damage are inadvertent.

Besides the requirements of *mala in se* that apply to everyone in a given society, contracts made in the proper form must be respected by those who are party to them. Also, every society has a large category of rules or regulations that are made to facilitate the smooth coexistence of cohabitants in matters that are intrinsically morally indifferent. In many cases, it doesn't matter for the most part precisely how things are done in a society provided that everyone does them in the same way. So, for example, there is no particular moral status attached to driving either on the right or the left side of the road but on busy roads where traffic moves at high speeds it is expedient that everyone drive either on the right or on the left.[38] This is not an area in which creative differences can be permitted. Things that are prohibited in this way are said to be *mala prohibita*.

In his typology of law A. John Simmons distinguishes five categories, the first two of which correspond to things *mala in se* or *mala prohibita*.[39] Simmons remaining three types of law are either (a) laws prohibiting private conduct that is nonaggressive but morally disapproved of by a section of the community or by the community at large, (b) laws relating to matters deemed necessary to protect the state such as laws prohibiting treason or requiring military service or (c) laws requiring payments to the state or permitting confiscation of property to fund state operations. Simmons regards laws in the area of *mala in se* and *mala prohibita* as the kind of thing that any society would require and it is difficult to disagree with him on this. From a libertarian perspective, however, the other three types of law he lists are out of bounds. Nonaggressive actions, however repulsive they may be deemed by some, may not be the subject of legal prohibition. If a state uses force to coerce its citizens to protect it (say by means of conscription) then it is in the same position as any other moral agent who engages in kidnapping, except that it does it on a grander scale.

And as we have already argued, taxation and confiscation are morally equivalent to theft.

Systems of customary law tend to converge on natural law, that is, the natural order of the world in which human beings live together. The key principle of natural law is justice, which is a disposition to give others their due, either negatively, by avoiding acts that are *mala in se*, or positively, by performing the requirements of contracts. Customary law then is not a set of commands issuing from some authority whereas this is precisely what legislation is – commands issued by a ruler, whether an individual or a group.[40] Typically, a piece of legislation, a statute, is drafted by civil servants on the direction of the cabinet or executive power, legislated by a parliament or house of congress after a debate which, in a modern democracy, is tightly controlled by the dominant government party, promulgated by a king, queen or president and enforced by the state-controlled police and state courts. The citizens in latter-day democracies have little or no say in this legislation and their only function is to obey it, ultimately under threat of the imposition of penalties. At best, they have the power to change one particular group of legislators for another at specified intervals but they have no power to reject the whole framework of legislators entirely.

What justification can there be for legislation? Insofar as it conforms to the justice required by natural law it is otiose while if it diverges from the justice required by natural law it is likely to be a law prohibiting nonaggressive but morally disapproved of conduct, a law delineating some offence against the state or a law permitting the state to appropriate your property. If the law is intended to change by force behaviour of which the legislators disapprove, that is, to impose a particular moral or economic policy on the people at large, it seeks to substitute the opinions of the legislators for those of the social participants themselves, presumably on the basis that the legislators know what is good for the people more than the people themselves do. But however well intentioned legislators may be (and I hope I may not be thought excessively cynical if I believe that they may not always be well-intentioned) they lack the requisite knowledge of the dispersed information that is required to make the best decisions, whether moral or economic, and so what the legislators promulgate merely reflects their subjective preferences.

In drawing a sharp contrast between legislation and law I do not want to be taken either as demonizing the contents of legislation or romanticizing the products of customary law. While attempting to give expression to the basic requirements of justice, customary law can fail to do so adequately and can embody individual and systematic biases. So too, it is possible for particular pieces of legislation (for example, statutes prohibiting homicide) to embody rules that are in fact perfectly acceptable in and of themselves. We are social animals and cannot but make our lives together; society is an order that emerges from human interaction and not a contractual construct; societies have within them, prior to legislation, a living, customary law which, while imperfect (beware – individual and group bias at work!) is broadly acquiesced in by those living in that society and different societies, while differing in some respects, can be expected to have many jurisprudential features in common.

It simply would not work

An objection frequently made to the libertarian anarchism proposal is that it simply could never work. The objection maintains that even if the various theoretical objections could be met, it just would not be possible to have a functioning society operating on libertarian anarchist principles. How is a libertarian anarchist to meet this objection? Whatever is actual is possible so that if we could show that a society exists exemplifying a libertarian anarchist legal order then the doubt about its possible instantiation would be significantly diminished. In what follows, I give a brief account of some societies whose legal systems *approximate* to that which was sketched earlier in the chapter.

It is important to make clear at the very start that I am *not* claiming that these societies are examples of pure libertarian anarchism. There are many things about them that a libertarian anarchist would find objectionable, not least the status restrictions on freedom of action and a tendency to subordinate the individual to the family or kinship group, but all that is needed for my purposes is to show that there have been societies that functioned without a state apparatus. In trying to do this it might be considered that I am pushing on an open door, for even Francis Fukuyama remarks that all over the world for most of human history people owed obligations 'not to a state but to kinfolk, they settle disputes not through courts but through a system of retributive justice . . .'.[41] Even so, given the iron grip of the present on our imaginations, I believe it is still worthwhile to see some examples of anarchic or quasi-anarchic legal orders in action.[42]

The Eskimo

'The Eskimo is what some would call an anarchist. He has no government in the formal sense, either over a territory or at all. There is no preëminent center of authority.'[43] Such is the opinion of the anthropologist E. Adamson Hoebel in his treatment of the Eskimo[44] in his seminal 1954 book *The Law of Primitive Man*. In the middle of the twentieth century, there were about 20,000 Eskimos spread thinly along a six thousand mile long Arctic fringe of North America. They lived in local groups of about one hundred persons in a dozen or so families and no larger social structures supervened upon these groups. A striking difference between Eskimo society and most other archaic societies is the almost complete unimportance, indeed absence, of kinship groups other than the immediate nuclear family. 'Kinship, except within very close degrees, is not emphasized, and as a result there is but little institutionalization of the extended family. . . . this makes Eskimos one of the most genuinely primitive groups known to

anthropologists.'[45] The clan or sept or tribe central to the functioning
of most other archaic societies is conspicuous by its absence.

All natural resources are available to be used by anyone who can
make use of them. There is no notion of property in land or territory,
not even communal property, still less private property so that no
group, even one resident in and using a particular area, can exclude
another group from that area. 'Eskimo interest is in game per se; land
is ignored and therefore not conceptualized as property.' Property
is recognized to exist in material objects that have been created or
personally used by individuals or in game that has been captured.
Despite this, a kind of Lockean spoilage proviso is applied to the
possession of game or personal objects so that 'no man can have
more than he can effectively use. . . . It is the giving away of food and
goods, not the possession of them, that wins honor and leadership
among the simple Eskimos'.[46]

In interpersonal relations, predictability is valued and aggression is
to be channelled and limited. In cases of non-sanctioned homicide,
such as murder, the family of the murder victim is expected to
execute blood revenge on the wrongdoer. Where someone engages
in repeated acts of unjustified killing, he becomes a public menace
and so the task of dealing with him falls not to a specific individual
but to the community as a whole. The one who is chosen or who
decides to execute sentence seeks and is granted prior approval by
the community at large so that his act will be legitimate and so not one
for which blood revenge can be sought.

The Eskimos acknowledge no government. Some individuals,
headmen, acquire a leadership role through their personal qualities
but this role is charismatic and not institutional. The headman is not
elected or chosen – he is someone whose judgement is respected
because of his wisdom. The Eskimo legal system is one of the most
rudimentary that can be imagined; it has no government or courts, no
policemen and such law as they have is manifested in their practices
and orally communicated. Despite this, Eskimo society is stable
'channelling human behavior, buttressing the control dikes along the

channels with primitive legal mechanisms, or their equivalents. . . . a social system is shaped in accordance with the social principles and values laid down in the basic postulates held by the members of Eskimo society'.[47]

I should not like to be understood to be taken as recommending that we adopt the values and practices of Eskimo society. The limitations and weaknesses of the system not to mention its specific formation by and adaptation to the material circumstances of Eskimo life are obvious. However, despite its limitations and imperfections, it shows that it is possible to organize a society without top-down government direction.

Early Irish society

In libertarian accounts of the viability of anarchism it is not unusual to point to Medieval Ireland[48] as an example of a society that functioned successfully for a substantial period of time without coercive central government.[49] The *tuath* was the basic territorial unit in medieval Ireland. There were approximately 150 of these *tuatha* in the whole country, each ruled over by a king (*ri*). The population of Ireland at this period was about 500,000 with, approximately, 3,000 people per *tuath*. The king, as the wealthiest and most powerful man in the neighbourhood, was central to the affairs of the *tuath*. All free men owed him loyalty and he could call upon them to repel invaders or to attack a neighbouring *tuath*. He also had the power to convene an *oenach* (a fair) for political, social and commercial purposes or an *aireacht* (meeting of freemen) at which legal business was transacted. Freemen generally stayed within their own *tuath*; only the professionals normally travelled outside the *tuath's* borders. The large degree of legal uniformity suggests that the *tuath's* lawyers kept in close touch with their colleagues in other *tuatha*. The king[50] was responsible for treaty-making, treaties of this kind being confirmed at an *oenach*. Under such treaties, a victim of a crime in one *tuath* committed by a member of another was entitled to legal redress. Crimes that were redressable included homicide, rape, wounding and robbery with violence, theft, housebreaking, arson and satire.

The kin-group (*derbfine*), all those descended from the same great grandfather, exercised legal powers over its members. Each kin-group had its own land; an individual's share in such common land could not be alienated contrary to the wishes of the rest of the group. It was possible to own land outside the kin-group and such land could be alienated freely. The kin-group was, in certain circumstances, responsible for the crimes and debts of its members, being obliged to pay the debts or fines of one who absconded after judgement. The body fine (*eraic*)[51] due when a member of a kin-group had been illegally killed was payable to the kin-group. The head of a kin-group was chosen, largely on the basis of his wealth, rank and demonstrated good sense.

While many early law codes in other societies were instigated by powerful kings 'there is little evidence of royal involvement in the composition of the Old Irish law-texts'.[52] In fact, the law and its formulation seems to have been the preserve of a special class of practitioners, more or less dispersed through the whole country, and not under the control of any king. Kelly attributes this low- or non-involvement of the kings in the law-making process to what he terms the 'political fragmentation' of the country at the time of their composition or redaction, clearly seeing this as a negative point and assuming, without grounds for so doing, a prior state of non-fragmentation. Kings could, however, issue emergency legislation (after defeat in battle or in the presence of a plague). If the king was not routinely involved in law-making, neither was he involved in law-implementation. This was done by means of a tort-like process involving suretyship, pledging and distraint.

Irish society in the historic period up to the seventeenth century constitutes one of the best examples of a functioning anarchic society. Irish law was the product of a body of private and professional jurists (called *brithim* or brehons) and was flexible and capable of development in response to evolving social conditions.[53] Law was a (largely) family business, enjoying high status. It is important to note that Irish law did not differentiate between tort and criminal law, in this respect resembling most systems of customary law that seem to come late, if at all, to this distinction. From the point of view of traditional law, crimes against the person tend to be regarded a special kind of offence against property.

The jurists gave judgement but the enforcement of those judgements was effected via a system of sureties. Sureties came in three forms: a surety might guarantee payment by pledging his enclann (honour price); or a surety could pledge his person and freedom; or the surety could guarantee the payment in the case of default. As Peden puts it, 'Law and order, and the adjustment of conflicting interests, were achieved through the giving of sureties rather than State-monopolized coercion.'[54]

Irish society, organized on these quasi-anarchical principles, lasted from about 500 BC to 1600 AD During those two thousand years it showed a capacity, vital to any organic and developing system of social organization, to absorb alien elements and internalize them. The Brehon Law was adapted by the English/Norman invaders or settlers, despite repeated attempts to dissuade them (e.g. by means of the Statutes of Kilkenny), so much so that, to the disgust of the English authorities, they became more Irish than the Irish themselves. The Irish legal system came to an end only when native Irish society collapsed after the Battle of Kinsale and the Flight of the Earls in the early seventeenth century. It ended, not as the result of insupportable internal strains, but as a consequence of external assault.

The Somalis

The Somali people make up a nation that, for most of its history, has operated on the basis of folk or customary law, applied and interpreted by judges.[55] This pattern of rule by judges, kritarchy,[56] a mode of social organization that was at one time found almost everywhere, was interrupted for a period when a form of statehood was adopted under colonial influence bringing with it the usual paraphernalia of legislatively created statute law. However, in 1991 the central governing structure of Somalia, first established in 1960, collapsed and the Somalis returned for the most part to their customary law. Most countries in Europe have mirrored the move from folk or customary law to state-sponsored legislation but, unlike the Somali, none has as yet returned to its previous legal order. The Somali case is, then, particularly apt as an example of a contemporary society functioning under the aegis of customary law where the modern template of statehood with its directorial executive and legislative body has been tried and rejected.

As with the ancient Irish system of law, the Somali legal order has no executive and no legislature. The basic pattern of Somali law and its administration follows the pattern of customary law found elsewhere in the world and exhibits the same quasi-universal characteristics including, especially, the rejection of the idea that it is proper for some to rule and others to be ruled. Law and government are quite distinct. The Somalis have an assembly (*guurti*) that is made up of the head of the most important among the families. It can decide on war and peace but cannot conscript or employ military personnel. While the assembly has no power to legislate or to overturn judgements of the courts, it can make recommendations. No votes are taken in this assembly. Discussion continues until a consensus is reached. Somali society and its legal structures are organized around kinship groups at various levels of size and complexity. This form of social organization by means of kinship groups based on common descent, real or nominal, was for most of human history the most ubiquitous mode of arranging for the orderly and peaceful operation of human affairs. It survived in the West until the last vestiges of it disappeared with the destruction of the Scottish clans in the eighteenth century.

The indigeneous system of Somali law is called *xeer*. *Xeer* must be considered to be law by the normal standards by which customs and conventions are considered to be law. The rules of *xeer* are known, are comprehensible, are consistent, dynamically stable and capable of being complied with, and bear on fundamental matters of life, liberty and property. *Xeer* is found intact in northern and western areas of Somalia though in some form or other it can be found everywhere throughout Somalia. It can be either general (*xeer guud*) and apply to everyone regardless of particular agreements or special (*xeer tolnimo*) and be dependent on specific and local arrangements. Xeer is independent of politics and, for the most part, of religion. The judge (*oday*), an elder who is normally the head of his own family, is expected to find the law not in the edicts of some ruler or political authority but in the standards of conduct that are to be found in the lived experience of the community. If a judge's verdicts are seriously at odds with these standards of conduct he will not find himself in demand. People are free to settle their disputes by agreement if they so choose and, besides the *xeer*, associations of various kinds have their own rules and regulations and where parties to a dispute are members of the same association, the dispute can be settled by reference to the rules of that association if the parties to the dispute agree to this procedure. *Xeer* is a living law and convergence between what is acceptable to different *xolos* and *jilibs* (extended families) is the norm.

In a manner similar to the system in ancient Irish law and in the law of other archaic societies, Somalis are insured against liabilities that they might incur through violation of the *xeer*. This insurance, in the form of sureties, is provided by their *jilib*. Those who show repeated disrespect for the law and are not susceptible to reformation of their conduct by means of family pressure can be 'uninsured' by their *jilib* and become, in effect, outlaws. Like most systems of customary law, the *xeer* of the Somalis has defects and limitations. *Xeer* prohibits homicide and assault but accepts killing in wartime. The basic rule is that for a life taken, a life must be given. It matters little whether the homicide is intentional or accidental. However, in most cases, the blood price of the victim (*mag*)[57] is acceptable.

Earlier in this chapter, in my story of the emergence of law, I sketched a situation in which two parties were in dispute but unable to agree bilaterally on its resolution, requiring the intervention of a third party to avoid violence. In Somali law, this is more or less what happens when a dispute arises between members of the same clan. Here, there is the added complication that each party in the dispute seeks aid from his family group. This aid will be solely defensive since the groups are unwilling to engage in pre-emptive hostile action against each other given that all families in a clan have kinship connections with one another and so might find themselves in a position of attacking a member of their kin. A situation will then be reached where two groups of more of less equal strength find themselves in a stalemate. To break the stalemate, recourse is had to a mediator whose job it is to settle the dispute as amicably and as peaceably as possible without that mediator having any power of direct enforcement. A non-arbitrary settlement can be obtained only if the judgement of the mediator is in accord with the communally accepted theory of justice. Such a theory will have emerged in the context of previous dispute resolution and will be based on property rights, whether the property in question is a person or the exterior goods belonging to that person. If a judgement is to be non-arbitrary and so acceptable to the community at large, it must be universalizable – what holds for A holds for B as well since, in respect of their fundamental rights, A and B are identical. This procedure is used not only for intra-clan disputes but also for inter-clan disputes. In this legal system, there is no place for any kind of political class division between rulers and ruled. The Somalis tell stories that uncannily mirror the advice relayed from God through Samuel to the Israelites when they asked for a king so that they could be like other nations instead of continuing in their kritarchic state. Unlike the Hebrews, the Somalis decided wisely against having a king![58]

Characteristics of customary legal systems

Ancient Irish law exhibited the following characteristics: the possession of property, with its rights and duties, was central to one's legal standing; there was no substantive distinction between criminal law and tort law; the legal system was private, customary, evolutionary and consensual; justice was primarily restorative, with restitution going to the victims rather than to a state; enforcement operated via a system of sureties and pledges, the ultimately recalcitrant being excluded from society and its protections.[59] With the possible exception of the property element, the same list can be drawn from the Somali system of law. Summarizing Leopold Pospisil's study of the legal system of the Kapauku people of New Guinea, Bruce Benson lists the following as its characteristics: primary rules bearing upon individual rights and property; law enforcement as the primary responsibility of the victim or victims; methods of adjudication in place to prevent if possible violent resolution of disputes; offences treated as wrongs against individuals (torts) not as offences against the state (crimes); economic sanctions as the primary method of punishment; strong incentives to yield to the decisions of adjudicators based on the threat of ostracism or exclusion from the community; the law of the community as a dynamically evolving expression of community norms.[60]

It is important to be clear that neither ancient Irish society nor present day Somali society nor any other historical illustration is given as an example of a libertarian paradise. It is easy, all too easy, to be an anthropo-legal functionalist and to think that whatever norms a group evolves are necessarily in order as they are. As we saw in the case of Somali law, this is not necessarily so. Methods of social control must, in the end, be subject to rational evaluation. However, without subscribing wholeheartedly to any form of anthropo-legal functionalism, I think it not unreasonable to conclude that customary laws that were wildly at variance with human needs, desires and interests would not long survive. 'Those customs and legal institutions that survive are relatively efficient because the evolutionary process is one of "natural selection," where laws or procedures that serve social interaction relatively poorly are ultimately replaced by improved laws and procedures.'[61] This, however, is merely a minimal requirement and there can be no guarantee that the customary laws of any society arrived at over time are maximally productive of the happiness of its members.

The disadvantages of the customary law systems considered include the following: they provide insufficient protection for certain categories of people, for example, women and strangers; they interfere with human freedom by restricting free speech by means of laws against defamation and blasphemy; they subordinate individuals to their kinship groups. The advantages of the customary law systems considered include the following: they are divorced from state politics, requiring no expensive standing military or quasi-military forces and permitting no monopoly courts to dominate the administration of law; unlike legislative systems, they are not capricious but nonetheless are dynamic; even taking into account the inevitable distortions that human weakness and bias introduce into them, their tendency is always to be an expression, albeit an imperfect one, of the basic order that is natural to human beings living together in society; they are effective; they require no coercive extraction of funds from the population to support them; they make restitution rather than punishment their purpose, thereby keeping clearly in mind that crimes are not committed against a state but against other human beings; they are consistent with and respect human freedom. Customary law is not a static mass of statutes but rather an evolutionarily adaptive legal system that is *not* the expression of the arbitrary will of the rulers of a society. The core of such systems is sound and capable of being adapted to contemporary mores and needs.

In a libertarian legal code, custom and traditional practice could not be the ultimate criteria of what the law would be. Any such law code would have to be based on the principle of non-aggression with elaborated principles of property rights and rules of evidence. Some may doubt that any stable and consistent law code could be constructed on libertarian principles; Murray Rothbard disagrees, noting that 'Not only are [libertarian law codes] *possible*, but over the years the best and most successful parts of our legal system were developed precisely in this manner.' In contrast, 'Legislatures, as well as kings, have been capricious, invasive, and inconsistent. They have only introduced anomalies and despotism into the legal system.' He concludes, 'government is no more qualified to develop and apply law than it is to provide any other service; and just as religion has been separated from the State and the economy can be separated from the State, so can every other State function, including police, courts, *and* the law itself!'[62]

Anarchy today

It may be objected that the examples I have given are either of no longer existent societies or societies that are utterly marginal in the modern world. Critics of libertarian anarchistic theory have not been slow to point out that Medieval Ireland is dead and gone, so too Medieval Iceland, and who, they wonder, would want to live in present day Somalia? 'It is all very well to point to historical or marginal instances of anarchic order', they might ask, 'but what has anarchy done for us recently?' This objection has some rhetorical force in that it seems to show the irrelevance of such considerations in the modern world but it doesn't affect the point of the examples, which is to show that an anarchic legal order is possible. However, given its rhetorical force, it might be useful to consider whether or not we can detect any current instantiations of anarchic orders. Perhaps surprisingly, the answer is yes.

The first and most obvious example of an existent anarchic legal order is the anarchy of international relations between states. Despite the efforts of the United Nations to act as if it were a world government it is not in fact a world government and states relate to one another, sometimes violently but for the most part cooperatively, in a context in which there is no ultimate legal or political arbiter of their disputes with one another. There are no global judges or policemen.[63]

Another example of existent anarchy perhaps somewhat surprisingly, is the operation of the state itself, or at least those states that are not pure autocracies. Within the governing apparatus of the state, its various elements – administrative, legal, executive and legislative – compete and cooperate with each other. If it should be objected that this takes place within the confines of a constitution, it can hardly have escaped anyone's notice that constitutions are not self-interpreting and their presence simply moves the intra-state anarchy on to another level.[64] 'The State functions according to voluntarily-made and enforced contracts without the need for violence from an authoritative third party. These are anarchic principles! It is delightfully ironic that the greatest example of anarchy working wonderfully in practice is within the State apparatus itself.'[65]

In the early 1990s, Tom Bell wrote a paper that was primarily an attempt to provide a theoretical justification for non-statist legal systems, for which he adopted the term 'polycentric law', its subcategories being customary law and privately produced law. Around the same time, Bell published a paper on the same topic in the *Human Studies Review* and still later, a short paper on practical applications in a Cato *Policy Report*.[66] He notes that once one becomes familiar with the notion of polycentric law, one sees instances of it everywhere – in churches, clubs, businesses and so on. Without the focusing lens of the concept, polycentric law is largely invisible. Although he provides a concise account of some historical examples of polycentric legal systems, Bell notes that a justification of polycentric law requires more than case studies of small and/or insular societies; it requires a justification for how polycentric law would work here and now. Following Benson, he isolates six features common to most systems of customary law, the first five of which would likely be mirrored in systems of privately produced law. Modified slightly, these are that (a) individual rights and private property take centre stage; (b) victims are the (ultimate) enforcers of the law; (c) violence is avoided by the emergence of standard (and, I would add, mutually agreeable) adjudicative procedures; (d) restitution/reparation (primarily economic) would follow from treating offences as torts (invasions of personal rights) rather than crimes (offences against the state); (e) the enforcement mechanism is ostracism, blackballing, blacklisting, banishment, exclusion from society; and (f) legal change comes about by evolution rather than by (legislative) revolution. One can immediately see that these features are strikingly characteristic of the customary legal systems discussed above, not necessarily in every respect but in their principal features.

Much of the resistance to libertarian anarchic proposals stems from a genuine inability on the part of one's audience to entertain such proposals as serious alternatives to the status quo. To be able to demonstrate convincingly to that audience that what one is proposing has already been done and continues to be done, albeit in different historical circumstances or in a variety of not-so-obvious ways, cannot but have a salutary effect on the receptivity of that audience to the theoretical arguments.

The importance of the historical examples of functioning anarchic societies and the contemporary evidence of functionally anarchic elements in statist societies is, among other things, to emphasize the sheer contingency of what seems like a necessity – to show that it wasn't always like this, that it is not like this everywhere or in every respect even now, and that it doesn't have to be like this. Bruce Benson, in the second chapter of *The Enterprise of Law*, shows clearly that the system of criminal law that we now possess – state legislatures,[67] public prosecution, prisons, juries, crimes against the State, public police forces – all of which seem as if they sprang, like Aphrodite, fully armed from the head of Zeus, are merely historically contingent developments. The pressure for these developments came not from any perceived increase in efficiency but from motives that were far less noble.

6
DELEGITIMIZING THE STATE

Try this experiment. Walk up to the proverbial man in the street and order him to perform some task, let us say, to touch his toes without bending his knees. It is always possible that your order might be obeyed – people are strange – but it is much more likely that you will receive a colourfully expressed answer. The purpose of this experiment (which you should not try unless you are feeling lucky) is to show that unless two people are part of a command structure such as an army, or are related as employee to employer, or connected by status (as children are to parents) an arbitrary command by one to the other is unlikely to be voluntarily obeyed. If you were to put a gun to the man in the street's head, your chance of getting him to touch his toes instead of his giving you cheek is greatly increased but his obedience to your command is clearly nonvoluntary and is mere acquiescence in *force majeure*. It is true that most well brought up people will voluntarily comply with some commands in the interests of social harmony ('Would you mind moving up a seat so that my friend and I can sit together?') provided that these commands are politely expressed, involve no great cost and, all things considered, are reasonable. In contrast, if you are ordered to do something brusquely by someone without authority, the natural reaction is bloody-mindedly to refuse to comply with the order unless you feel intimidated, in which case we are back to *force majeure*.[1]

The state is an organization in which the systematic exercise of command by some over others is ultimately backed by the allegedly legitimate use of violence. This structure of command requires justification. All states distinguish between rulers who issue commands and the ruled who are obliged to obey them; the interesting question is – who should occupy the position of ruler and who the position of the ruled? In the contemporary world, representative democracy is the only plausible contender for legitimizing the state and the major selling point of representative democracy is the notion of political representation. The basic idea is that in a *representative* democracy the people rule themselves via their representatives and so the awkward gap between rulers and ruled is bridged.[2] Everything depends on the notion of political representation making sense. If it doesn't, the ability of representative democracy to legitimize the state becomes problematic. In the first part of this chapter I will argue that the notion of political representation is vacuous and so to the extent that the legitimacy of the state depends upon its supposed ability to represent those whom it rules the state is not legitimate.

From another perspective, the existence and operation of the modern state is sometimes justified on the grounds that it is based upon a constitution, that constitution supposedly being the source of both the political authority of the state and its minions and the political obligations of the citizen. A number of questions immediately spring to mind. What are constitutions and where do they come from? More significantly, why are constitutions considered to be authoritative?[3] My argument in the second part of this chapter in brief is this: a constitution is either a contract or it is not. If it is a contract, it is either explicit or implicit. I will try to show that constitutions are not and, except in the most unusual circumstances, cannot be explicit contracts. The alternative (and much more commonly held) position that constitutions are implicit or tacit contracts is said to be warranted by our voting in elections or by our residing within a given geographical area or by our payment of taxes or by other similar modes of conduct. I will argue that none of these modes of conduct suffices to make constitutions into contracts. If constitutions are *not* contracts, it might still be held that they are nonetheless binding and authoritative. A defence of this contention appears to rest upon a conception of society as a whole as a kind of family-writ-large which embodies, in the political arena, the pre-contractual status relationships that are constitutive of the family. According to this account, the political authority of the state and the political obligation of the citizen, then, would be pre-contractual and a-consensual. I argue that this defence of the authority of constitutions, while perhaps music to the ears of some conservative thinkers, is radically implausible.

Making the world safe *from* democracy[4]

Tom Hanks and Passepartout are the only two human inhabitants of a Pacific island.[5] Neither is aware of the existence of the other until, one fateful day, they meet. What happens next is a matter of some moment. Will they greet each other politely and go about their respective businesses? Will they agree to cooperate for their mutual benefit? Will they fight? Who can tell? However, we can be reasonably sure in supposing that if Hanks were to command Passepartout to 'Tote dat barge! Lif' dat bale!', or demand that Passepartout give up his vile habit of drinking coconut juice while eating fish, or insist that Passepartout cooperate with him in his fishing and hunting ventures or abstain from servile work on a Sunday – in short, if Hanks were in any way to attempt to require Passepartout to obey his commands, Passepartout would, I believe, rightly resent, and probably resist, such injunctions. The same, of course, would apply if roles were to be reversed and Passepartout were to assume the position of would-be commander. The Hanks-Passepartout scenario can be replicated in any number of literary variations, limited only by the fertility of one's imagination. For example, more people might be added to the island's population and, while this would result in there being more possible relationships, it would not change the nature of those relationships.

The essential principles regarding the legitimacy of command[6] can be established by reflection on our insular drama and can be expressed in the following six propositions:

---

(1) Outside of freely arrived at binding agreements between them, Andrew may legitimately command Benjamin to refrain from action C if and only if C is a demonstrable initiation of aggression against the person or property of Andrew or against the person or property of another innocent human being.

(2) Andrew may legitimately command Benjamin to perform action C if and only if C is an element of a freely (non-coercively) arrived at binding agreement between Andrew and Benjamin, and C is not a demonstrable initiation of aggression against the person of property of another human being.

(3) In no other circumstances may Andrew legitimately command Benjamin.

(4) If, in (1), Benjamin refuses to refrain from the action C, then Andrew may use proportionate force to restrain or punish him.

(5) If, in (2), Benjamin refuses to perform action C, Andrew may use proportionate force to elicit compensation or specific performance from Benjamin.

(6) If, outside situations (1) and (2) Andrew commands Benjamin, Benjamin may refuse to comply.

What is true of the one is true of the many so that if no one person has a right to command another except under the conditions specified, no two persons acting severally or in concert have that right. They may, of course, combine to use their superior force to coerce another into doing what they command but that is a matter of might, not right. Whether the number of people purporting to command another be one, two, seven, one thousand two hundred and twenty three, or ten million, it cannot, except under the conditions sketched above, be a matter of right.

'We're on a mission from God!'

In every modern state, some group of people, usually a fairly small group, claims to have the authority to command the rest of the population to do this or that or to refrain from doing this or that. They usually do not possess such a right by virtue of their manifestly superior intelligence or moral character since sad experience shows that our erstwhile leaders, by and large, are no better in general than the rest of us and are often, sadly, much worse. Clarence Darrow is scathing in his evaluation of the moral character of our erstwhile rulers, declaring that they have been 'conspicuous for all those vices that they so persistently charge to the common people' so that if there is any group of people from whose depredations society needs to be saved 'it is those same rulers who have been placed in absolute charge of the lives and destinies of their fellow men'.[7] By what right, then, do they claim the authority to command us, to make laws for us that govern many, if not most, of the significant aspects of our lives? Why are *they* entitled to call upon *us* to refrain from taking government non-approved drugs or driving without seat belts or to pay the taxes they demand or to serve in their armed forces and fight their wars?

In the not so distant past, those who claimed the right to govern others did so because they had, they claimed, a mandate from God (rather like the Blues Brothers but with ambitions extending beyond the limits of Cook County) or were better than the common run of man by virtue of their outstanding intellects, sterling characters, Nietzschean will or distinguished family tree or had more money than the peasantry; or were simply more powerful than most other people. Whatever persuasive character such justifications may have had in the past, they have none now. Divine Rule theories of government are at an all-time low ebb in the intellectual market, aristocratic theories of government command no respect, oligarchic theories even less and 'might is right' theories are now, as they have always been, absolutely bankrupt. In the arena of governmental justification democracy is the only game in town, for if there is a fundamental article of faith in the contemporary world it is not that God is dead or that soccer is the beautiful game; it is, rather, that democracy is a GOOD THING, so good, in fact, that the whole world must be given it whether the whole world wants it or not. Fukuyama believes that in the twentieth century the idea that 'democracy was the most, or indeed the only, legitimate form of government spread to every corner of the world'.[8] In fact, as Michael Bakunin noted, democracy is a form of oligarchy that differs from 'normal' oligarchy only inasmuch as the oligarchs change from time to time. That our erstwhile representatives change from time to time does not, of course, 'prevent the formation . . . of a body of politicians, privileged in fact though not in law, who, devoting themselves exclusively to the direction of the public affairs of a country, finally form a sort of political aristocracy or oligarchy'.[9]

Democracy and representation

The key to the justification and popular acceptance of democracy is the idea of representation: those who are ruled are thought to be ruled by those who represent them and thus, it is claimed, in being so ruled they are, in effect, virtually ruling themselves. Consider the following passage from Hobbes:

> For he that doth anything by authority from another, doth therein no injury to him by whose authority he acteth: But by this Institution of a Common-wealth every particular man is Author of all the Soveraigne doth; and consequently he that complaineth of injury from his Soveraigne complaineth of that whereof he himself is Author, and therefore ought not to accuse any man but himselfe; no, nor himselfe of injury, because to do injury to ones selfe is impossible.[10]

If rulers and ruled are virtually one and the same, then the problem of justifying one person's or group of people's arbitrarily commanding another disappears. Whatever difficulties there might be about the legitimacy of another person commanding you, there can be no disputing the legitimacy of your commanding yourself. Whether the notion of commanding yourself (as distinct from the notion of self-command) makes any sense is another matter. The justification of political governance by the state, then, rests upon democracy, and the justification of democracy in turn rests upon representation. If the bough of representation were to break, down would come the cradle of democracy, baby and all. Somewhat less metaphorically, if representation cannot be satisfactorily accounted for then representative democracy as the sole viable contender for the justification of political governance by the state finds itself in no more tenable a position than any of its discredited competitors.

The classic work on representation is Hanna Pitkin's *The Concept of Representation*, now over 40 years old.[11] She supports my claim regarding the linkage of democracy and representation, noting, '. . . the contemporary popularity of the concept [of representation] depends much upon its having become linked with the idea of democracy . . .'[12] although, as she points out correctly, '[i]nitially, neither the concept nor the institutions to which it was applied were linked with elections or democracy . . .'.[13] Given this contemporary firm linkage between democracy and representation, how is one to conceive of political representation? Are political representatives the agents of those whom they represent, whose function as agents is limited to the carrying out of their principals' instructions? Or are they trustees, free to act in the interests of those whom they represent according to their own best judgement of what those interests are? Or are they neither agents nor trustees, being simply able to do more or less whatever they like once elected? Or are there other possibilities as well as these?

What is it to represent?

The idea of political representation derives such rhetorical force as it has from a set of loose analogies with non-problematic, mundane instances of representation, some of which I will sketch below. Unfortunately, none of the ordinary instances of representation translates without loss into the political realm and ultimately there is no coherent idea of political representation that can survive rational scrutiny.

What, if any, are the constraints on representation? One could envisage someone standing up at a shareholders' meeting and saying 'I represent the small investor and I believe that the entire Board of Directors should be removed' or in a University meeting, saying, 'I represent the administrative staff of the university and we want parity of treatment with the academic staff.' One may question whether or not such alleged representatives are in fact representative but their claim to be representatives of their constituencies seems in principle comprehensible even if it should turn out to be false. However, what would one make of someone standing up to say 'I represent myself and I believe the entire Board of Directors should be removed' or 'I represent myself and I demand parity of treatment with the academic staff of the university.' To put it at its lowest estimate, this use of 'represent' seems odd. Of course, one can imagine that in circumstances where it is customary or conventional for one to be represented by another (e.g. as a defendant in a legal trial) one might answer the question 'Who represents you?' when put to you by the judge by saying 'I am representing myself, my Lord.' Clearly, however, this claim is to be understood as equivalent to the perfectly sensible denial that anyone else is representing me rather than the dubiously meaningful claim that I am, in fact, representing myself. It would seem, then, that a minimal constraint on representation is that there should be a real distinction between the one representing and the one being represented.

In what way are political representatives *representative*?

What does it mean for one person to represent another? Under normal circumstances those who represent us do so at our bidding and cease to do so at our bidding. They act on our instructions within the boundaries of a certain remit and we are responsible for what they do as our agents. The central characteristic of representation by agency is that the agent is responsible to his principal and is bound to act in the principal's interest. Is this the situation with my so-called political representatives? Political representatives are not (usually) legally answerable to those whom they allegedly represent. In fact, in modern democratic states, the majority of a representative's putative principals are in fact unknown to him. Can a political representative be the agent of a multitude? This also seems unlikely. What if there are multiple principals and they have interests that diverge from each other? A political representative must then of necessity cease to represent one or more of his principals. The best that can be done in these circumstances is for the politician to serve the many and betray the few.[14] In this very normal political scenario, it is not that it is *difficult* to represent a constituency – it is rather that it is *impossible*.[15] There is no interest common to the constituency as a whole, or, if there is, it is so rare as to be practically non-existent. That being the case, there is nothing that can be represented.

Some may take issue with the notion of representation presented here and argue that we are dealing with a considerably more complex phenomenon, that political representation is just one instance of a variety of types of representation, that representation can be symbolic,[16] formal, religious[17] or iconic. Firstly, while my remarks apply primarily to representation-as-agency, similar considerations can be brought to bear on representation as trustee, deputy or commissioner and so on. Once again, as with our desert island drama, the basic conceptual point can be grasped from the single example of representation-as-agency – there is little to be gained, except a soothing tedium, from a rehearsal of the inapplicability of the other paradigmatic types to political representation.

Having exhaustively examined the various instances of unproblematic representation – agent, trustee, deputy, commissioner and so on – Pitkin regretfully concludes that none of them seems capable of carrying the burden that political representation must carry if it is to be adequately robust. The political representative 'is neither agent nor trustee nor deputy nor commissioner; he acts for a group of people without a single interest, most of whom seem incapable of forming an explicit will on political questions'.[18] It is difficult to see how this point could be made more clearly. One might perhaps think that such a state of conceptual confusion would lead one to give up any idea of discovering a coherent or consistent account of political representation but Pitkin ploughs on. She wonders if we should abandon the very idea of political representation and considers the possibility that 'representation in politics is only a fiction, a myth forming part of the folklore of our society'.[19] Even more radically, she wonders whether we should not 'simply accept the fact that what we have been calling representative government is in reality just party competition for office'.[20]

One is tempted to say – Yes! Yes! Alas, Pitkin says – No! No! She thinks that perhaps it is 'a mistake to approach political representation too directly from the various individual representation analogies – agent and trustee and deputy'[21] at one stroke abandoning her working assumption of a common semantic core lying at the heart of the notion of representation. Having abandoned the common core idea, she proceeds to suggest a kind of institutional or systemic account.

> Political representation is primarily a public, institutionalized arrangement involving many people and groups, and operating in the complex ways of large-scale social arrangements. What makes it representation is not any single action by any one participant, but the over-all structure and functioning of the system, the patterns emerging from the multiple activities of many people. It

is representation if the people (or a constituency) are present in governmental action, even though they do not literally act for themselves.[22]

Given what she has been urging up to this point, this recommendation is a counsel of despair. It comes to this. None of the paradigmatic uses of the term 'representation', as instanced by the various examples Pitkin considers (deputy, agent and so on) suffices to make sense of the idea of political representation so Pitkin invents a whole new unsubstantiated stipulative systemic account of representation that has no roots in our ordinary use of that term. Instead of individuals representing, we instead have an entire system that represents. We are to forget that we have been unable to make any sense of individual political representation; we can kick the problem upstairs by ignoring the individual and having the system itself be representative, albeit in a somewhat mysterious and yet-to-be explained way. Let us risk committing the fallacy of composition and assert that if the idea of explicating political representation by means of the analysis of individual acts of agency, trusteeship and so on is unrealizable, the problem is hardly solved by simply positing 'the system' as the super agent of representation. I would go further: the systemic account is not only unhelpful it is obfuscatory, appearing to explain when in fact it simply sweeps the problem under a pseudo-explanatory carpet in a manner reminiscent of the postulation of 'dormitive power' by the doctor in Moliere's *Le Malade Imaginaire* as an explanation of the soporific qualities of opium. This, of course, is to explain the obscure by the more obscure; it is also a striking example of what Alfred North Whitehead called 'The Fallacy of Misplaced Concreteness.'

If it is to be tenable, representative or indirect democracy requires a clear, robust and defensible conception of representation. No such conception has been forthcoming and it is doubtful if any ever will be forthcoming. It used to be said that only three things were definitely true of the Holy Roman Empire: it wasn't holy, it wasn't Roman and it wasn't an empire. Similarly, two things are definitely true of representative democracy: it is not democracy and it is not representative. In the end, representation is a fig leaf that is insufficient to cover the naked and brutal fact that even in our sophisticated modern states, however elegant the rhetoric and however persuasive the propaganda, some rule and others are ruled. The only question is, as Humpty-Dumpty noted in *Through the Looking-Glass*, '. . . which is to be master – that's all'.[23]

What are constitutions?
Where do they come from?

A constitution is a specific document that is considered to be the basic law of the state or, in the case of the United Kingdom, a set of documents embodying a mixture of legislation, case law together with conventions and customs, or, *in extremis*, the foundational customs and conventions upon which a society operates whether consigned to writing or not. Lon Fuller holds that customary law is constitutional law inasmuch as it 'involves the allocation among various institutions . . . of legal power, that is, the authority to enact rules and to reach decisions that will be regarded as properly binding on those affected by them'.[24]

The distinction between written and unwritten constitutions should not be exaggerated; as Hilaire Barnett notes, 'Under all constitutions, not all of the rules will be written, and still less will they be collected within a single document.'[25] A constitution generally sets out the structure of the organs of government, orders their relationships to each other and to the citizens of the state and may include a bill of rights or similarly functioning provisions, either integrally, or as a series of amendments or as an act of Parliament.[26] A constitution can be either a piece of paper with words on it, or 'the actual institutions, practices, and incentive structures'[27] that are operative in a society. Roderick Long describes as a 'metaphysical illusion' the idea that constitutional restraints exist somehow outside the society over which they are meant to be operative. No pattern of social organization is guaranteed to survive just by virtue of the brilliance of its structures; the dynamic process of social interaction will be more likely to be a success and survive if there are incentives to keep people acting in appropriate ways.

The really important question about constitutions is not so much what they are or even how states come to acquire them but why they are supposed to have the authority that is granted to them. Is a constitution a contract subsisting between the citizens of the state and their rulers; is it some other kind of (non-contractual) agreement or is it something completely *sui generis*? The possibilities would seem to be these: either a constitution is a binding agreement among a group of people to be governed in a particular way, or it is somehow binding but not the subject of an agreement.[28] If it is a binding agreement, there are two sub-possibilities – either it is an explicit agreement or an implicit or tacit agreement.

Are constitutions contracts?

It is not unusual for constitution-makers to represent the objects of their constructive activities as compacts, covenants or contracts. The Massachusetts Constitution of 1780, in its Preamble, claims that 'The body-politic is formed by a voluntary association of individuals: It is a social compact, by which the whole people covenants with each citizen, and each citizen with the whole people, that all shall be governed by certain laws for the common good.'[29]

The paradigm of the binding agreement is the contract. The standard view of a contract in the Common Law tradition is that it is not just any kind of agreement but one that possesses quite specific characteristics. Ordinary daily life is full of agreements that are ordinarily not taken to be contractual. Marilyn's failure to keep her date with

Joe is not, alas, something that renders her liable to be sued and if, in a moment of weakness I, as your friend, promise to read your draft novel but do not then our friendship may end but you are highly unlikely to recover damages from me in court. For something to be a contract, the agreement that forms its substance requires a valid offer and a valid acceptance of that offer and, despite challenges (from Lord Denning[30] – who else?) this would still appear to be the received view. The agreement can either be bilateral (an exchange of promises) or unilateral (where the one who makes the offer alone makes a promise, the acceptance of which consists in someone's doing what is set out in the offer). An offer, to be valid, must be communicated. The communication may be in writing, in speech or in conduct; it must be definite and it must be distinguished from a mere invitation to enter into negotiations. To be valid, the acceptance of an offer must be made while the offer is still operative by the person to whom the offer is made, must match the terms of the offer and may be written, oral or, in certain very specific circumstances, may be inferred from conduct and such acceptance must, of course, be communicated to the one making the offer.

Besides its offer-acceptance structure, contracts in the Anglo-American Common Law legal tradition also require that there be something in the arrangements to indicate that those making the promises intend to be bound by their agreement. A properly constituted deed[31] will be one such arrangement and if one were to believe Lord Denning (again!) promissory estoppel[32] would be another, but, these special cases to one side, consideration is the standard 'badge of enforceability' where consideration is defined as 'some right, interest, profit or benefit to one party' or 'some forbearance, detriment, loss or responsibility given, suffered or undertaken by the other'.[33]

In general, only the parties to a contact can sue or be sued on a contract.[34] There are exceptions to this limitation in respect of the assignment of rights, in the matter of agency, in trusts and in multipartite agreements, in some aspects of land law (restrictive covenants) as well as some statutory exceptions. Third parties can enforce a contractual provision of benefit to them where the contract expressly provides for third party benefit or where the contract is intended to provide third parties with legally enforceable rights. To the best of my knowledge, however, I know of no case where third parties (other than, say, principals in a principal–agent relationship) can be burdened by a contract to which they are not explicitly a party. This asymmetry of benefit and burden is particularly relevant in considering whether or not constitutions can be assented to implicitly or tacitly.

If political constitutions are to be construed as contracts we might well wonder what the offer is, what would constitute acceptance (or rejection), who is making the offer and who is accepting it, what the consideration is supposed to be and, finally, who is included within (or excluded from) the reach of the contract? Without much reflection, one can immediately grasp that there would be a great deal of difficulty in answering these questions in relation to any existent political constitution. Let us see how questions like these are capable of being answered in the case of one such constitution, the Constitution of the United States of America.

Constitutions as explicit contracts

Lysander Spooner (1808–87), the American lawyer, entrepreneur, abolitionist and protolibertarian political theorist, has no doubt that the US Constitution purports to be a contract, arguing that it can have no authority or obligation '*unless as a contract between man and man*'.[35] He believes that if the US Constitution is to have legal effect it must be a contract of some kind but that as it is not a contract (in any relevant sense); it has no inherent authority and imposes no obligations on the majority of US citizens.[36]

Who are the parties to the US Constitution? According to Spooner, the only possible candidates for these positions would be those people who were actually around at the time when it was approved. Does that mean that all the people living in the United States of

America eighty years before Spooner wrote his tract must be taken
to have been parties to the Constitution? No – only those people
legally entitled and competent to make contracts among those who
were alive at the time of its making are eligible for this distinction but
not even all of these were, in fact, parties to the Constitution for, as
Spooner notes: '. . . we know, historically, that only a small portion
even of the people then existing were consulted on the subject, or
asked, or permitted to express either their consent or dissent in any
formal manner.'[37] Needless to say, women and blacks were excluded
from the franchise completely and property qualifications excluded
anywhere from one half to three quarters of the white male adults. Of
the remaining small amount of potentially qualified voters, how many
actually exercised their franchise and gave their explicit assent to the
Constitution?

The US Constitution opens with the words: 'We, the people of the
United States . . . .' What is signified by this 'we'? Spooner believes
that it can only mean particular individuals, acting freely and voluntarily.
Such authority as the Constitution has, it has only between those who
actually consented and no one else.[38] He invites us to imagine another,
rather less grandiose, agreement, in which we might say, 'We, the
people of Philadelphia, [or London or Paris or Dublin] agree to maintain
a school. . . . for ourselves and our children.' Such an agreement
would, of course, be binding only on those who actually subscribed to
it and on the terms agreed and any attempt to compel those who had
not given their explicit consent to it to contribute to the maintenance of
the school would be a form of extortion. References to posterity have
no legal significance and cannot be taken to imply that there was any
acknowledgement of a right or power to bind posterity.

Only those who actually consented to the Constitution, whoever
they may have been and whatever their number may have been,
managed to bind themselves and no others were or are bound.
Since none of the original parties to the purported contract that is
the US Constitution was alive in 1870 when Spooner was writing,
he believes it follows that '. . . *the Constitution, so far as it was their*

contract, died with them. They had no power or right to make it
obligatory upon their children. It is not only plainly impossible, in the
nature of things, that they *could* bind their posterity, but they did not
even attempt to bind them'.[39]

In words eerily reminiscent of the US Constitution, the preamble
to *Bunreacht na hÉireann* (the Irish Constitution) reads: 'We, the
people of Eire . . . Do hereby adopt, enact, and give to ourselves
this Constitution.' We can raise two questions on this statement:
what action was being performed in this adoption, enactment and
self-giving of the Constitution and who, precisely, was performing this
action.

The answer to the second question would appear to be, the
people of Eire. All of them? Not exactly. In the plebiscite of 1 July
1937 1,346,207 people voted; given a total eligible electorate of
1,775,055, that amounted to a voting percentage of 76 per cent. Of
those who voted, the votes of no less than 134,157 were spoilt, almost
10 per cent! 685,105 voted in favour (51 per cent of those who voted;
39 per cent of the total electorate); 526,945 voted against (39 per cent
of those who voted; 30 per cent of the total electorate). Altogether,
those who voted against the ratification of *Bunreacht na hÉireann*,
those whose votes were spoiled, and those who refrained from voting
came to 1,089,950 – 61 per cent. That means that only 39 per cent
of all the eligible electors actually voted in favour of the measure. So,
the preamble should perhaps be amended to read, 'We, 39 per cent
of the eligible electorate of the people of Eire . . .' which doesn't quite
have the stirring resonance of the original.

By adopting, enacting and giving to themselves this document,
just what were (39 per cent of the eligible voters of) the people of
Éire doing? Who were they doing it for or to? Did they purport to
bind themselves to the provisions of this document? For how long
were they to be bound? And what of the 30 per cent who specifically
rejected this document, those whose votes were spoiled, those who
did not vote, those not eligible to vote and those not yet born – are
they to be bound by this document? If so, why? Clearly they have

given no formal assent to this document – their agreement to it has not
been explicitly given nor, in some cases, has it even been sought.

Constitutions as implicit contracts

Since no evidence of actual consent is forthcoming from the majority
of current citizens the claim that constitutions are authoritative has to
rest on some notion of implicit or tacit consent. The core of Hume's
celebrated attack on consent theory is essentially that the public
at large are wholly unconscious of the fact, if it is a fact, that actual
consent is required for the political legitimacy of their rulers and their
own political obligations or that can be deemed to have given implicit
consent to the legitimacy of their rulers by their continued residence
within the boundaries of Great Britain. Other means by which such
implicit consent is supposed to be made manifest are commonly taken
to be by the receipt of benefits from the state or voting in elections or
the payment of taxes.

Let us look at the residence argument first. The argument has often
been made against the necessity for explicit consent in all cases of
contract that there are well recognized circumstances in which we
can make binding agreements without engaging in any formalities.
I allowed above that some contracts can be formed by a course of
conduct, one of the most familiar of which is, perhaps, ordering a meal
in a restaurant. If William orders a meal in a restaurant and consumes
it, then he has incurred an obligation to pay for it; the lack of an explicit
verbal agreement does not relieve him of his monetary obligations. One
might imagine a visitor from a radically alien culture innocently failing to
realize this cultural and legal norm and thinking that he was witnessing
a gratuitous distribution of food with ensuing comical complications,
comical at least to onlookers if not to the mystified alien and the out-
of-pocket restaurateur.

Whatever may be the case in the relatively trivial and transient contractual situations engendered by the purchase of food in a restaurant and such like, in most jurisdictions one cannot form contracts in respect of significant assets, such as automobiles or houses that saddle one with significant obligations in the same casual existential manner. Randy Barnett notes that even for something as relatively trivial as the lease of a television most legal systems require a complete account of the obligations one is taking on in return for the benefits received. That being the case, he remarks on the irony of resting our duty to obey the law on such a slender reed as that of 'tacit consent' so that merely by living in a certain town or not leaving our country of birth 'we have "consented" to obey nearly any command that is enacted by the reigning legal system. And the consent of a majority is supposed to bind not only themselves, but dissenters and future generations as well'.[40]

While it is true that entering a marriage or making a will are activities that once were informally transacted, they have since come to be attended with a significant degree of formality so that one cannot now get married (even in Las Vegas) or make a will without being explicitly aware of just what it is one is doing. If such formality with its attendant explicit reflection and consent characterizes such important matters, how much more then is explicit reflection and explicit consent required in the matter of accepting a constitution, given that it purports to be the fundamental law by which one is to be bound?

Some, such as Hume,[41] have attempted to defuse the residency argument by arguing that for consent to be genuine, it must be voluntary and that in many cases the demand that people either stay and obey or leave presents people with alternatives neither of which they can really be said to choose. Hume instances the position of the unskilled peasant presented with such a choice and deems it to be equivalent to that of a man kidnapped and taken aboard a boat without his consent who is given the option of either consenting to the authority of the ship's master or jumping overboard. The choice is not simply to stay and obey or leave; one may also stay and not obey – a possibility that might have unpleasant consequences but is nonetheless an option. Attempts by the state to enforce obedience in matters not covered by the principle of non-aggression will then be coercive and those who remain will have a choice of whether to actively resist such aggression or to acquiesce in it in the face of *force majeure*, without such acquiescence being tantamount to any form of legitimation of the authority of the state to require such obedience.

The argument is sometimes made that those who receive benefits from a state, such as the provision of housing or healthcare, the use of roads and police services, tacitly accept the legitimate authority of that state by their acceptance of such benefits. In response to this argument it could be argued that such benefits, to the extent that they *are* actually benefits, could be regarded as positive externalities much as your neighbour's dazzling flower display is a welcome addition to the visual delights of your neighbourhood. And just as you would be surprised to receive a bill from your neighbour for the pleasure his flower display gives you and be rightly resistant to paying it, so too the benefits provided by the state being, as it were, happy accidents you can neither be legitimately charged for them nor required to submit to the authority of the state in return for them. After all, just as one may acquiesce passively in the negative elements of state action without thereby being taken to legitimate it, so too, one can similarly acquiesce in the positive elements of state action without legitimating consequences. Simmons remarks that most citizens 'not unreasonably take the public goods they receive to be fully "bought and paid for" (indeed, overpaid for) from governments with tax payments. Mandatory purchase of overpriced public goods with compulsory tax payments does not leave much to account for the alleged additional aspects of political obligation . . .'.[42]

It is sometimes claimed that because people can vote in elections organized by the state this is a tacit admission by them of the legitimacy of state authority. Is mere ability (that is, having a right) to vote enough to generate this legitimation? This seems radically implausible, confusing the possession of the opportunity to consent (if, indeed, it is that) with consent. Perhaps it will be claimed that by our having the right to vote we have the right to change the laws, including the constitution, of the state and thereby consent to the status quo?[43]

As a matter of fact, no individual citizen in a modern state has the right to change either the state's laws or its constitution. That can only be done by a majority in specific situations. If it is said that I have consented to the right of a majority to make the appropriate changes and am thereby bound, one could well ask how I am to be taken to have consented to *this* particular arrangement. It cannot be by voting in a situation in which a majority outcome is held to determine the choice of all, unless one wants to proceed in a viciously circular motion and justify majority decisions by a majority decision that has yet to be justified.

As a general principle, it is almost always dangerous to draw conclusions from non-action. It is only if a context is present in which non-action is clearly indicative of a choice that non-action can be taken to have positive implications. For the most part, such contexts will engender consequences that are relatively trivial. 'Inactivity that results from ignorance, habit, inability, or fear will not be a way of consenting to anything. Citizens of modern democracies are not continuously, or even occasionally, presented with situations where their inactivity would represent a clear choice of the status quo.'[44]

If the mere right to exercise the franchise is insufficient, what of actual exercise of that right? It might be said that in voting in a particular election one consents to the overall political context because, for the most part, one understands the context in which one is operating. So, when you vote for Smith you know that Smith is a member of the Help-Yourself-Party and that the HYP will, if they achieve a majority in Parliament, form a government and make laws and regulations for you and for others. If you know all this when you vote, then you consent to it all and thereby legitimize the political system as a whole.

It is highly probable that many people are in fact unaware of the larger political context when they vote and that even when they are so aware, in voting they are exercising a preference *within* a given political context the nature or even existence of which is not itself a matter of choice in this or in any other election. In these circumstances, voting is almost always simply a choice of the lesser of two evils, one or other of which is to be forced upon me and neither of which I would voluntarily choose if I had a more radical choice. If I hand over my wallet to a mugger rather than take the risk of physical assault it would be perverse to describe my act of transferring the wallet as being freely chosen and somehow a recognition of the legitimacy of mugging. If I do not want to support the particular form of state claiming dominion over me than to support in an election or, indeed, any state, that is not a choice I am being offered. I am being offered only a choice between whether A or B holds the levers of power, not whether or not there should be levers of power in the first place. Spooner denies that voting in a political system implies *de facto* consent to that system, remarking that without his having been asked for his opinion on the matter 'a man finds himself environed by a government that he cannot resist; a government that forces him to pay money, render service, and forego the exercise of many of his natural rights, under peril of weighty punishments'. He can either vote or not vote. He would prefer not to be in this situation, a situation that is not of his choosing but as things stand, vote or not vote he must. If he votes, 'his case is analogous to that of a man who has been forced into battle, where he must either kill others, or be killed himself. Because, to save his own life in battle, a man attempts to take the life of his opponents, it is not to be inferred that the battle is one of his own choosing'. Similarly, if a man should vote as a means of self-defence or self-preservation, that should not be taken to imply that he thereby approves and gives his consent to the whole enterprise.[45]

Taxes, being compulsory, their payment provides no evidence that taxpayers legitimize the constitution under the aegis of which the government of the day extracts those taxes. If taxes were voluntary then tax payers might by their voluntary contributions be said to support the activities of those receiving them, much as we might be said to support the activities of a charitable organization to which we voluntarily give money. But taxes are not voluntary; they are extracted by a threat of force. Spooner compares the tax collector to a highwayman, to the detriment of the tax collector. Unlike the tax collector, the highwayman 'does not pretend that he has any rightful claim to your money, or that he intends to use it for your own benefit. He does not pretend to be anything but a robber'. Unlike the tax collector, the highwayman 'has not acquired impudence enough to profess to be merely a "protector," and that he takes men's money against their will, merely to enable him to "protect" those infatuated travellers, who feel perfectly able to protect themselves, or do not appreciate his peculiar system of protection'. Yet again, having taken your money, the highwayman, unlike the tax collector, 'does not persist in following you on the road, against your will; assuming to be your rightful "sovereign," on account of the "protection" he affords you'. He doesn't insist on 'protecting' you whether you want to be protected or not nor would he take it as a personal insult if you were to resist his commands. As Spooner sardonically remarks 'He is too much of a gentleman to be guilty of such imposture, and insults, and villainies as these.'[46]

Despite its pretensions, Spooner concludes, the US Constitution is not a contract; it binds nobody, and those who claim to act by its authority are in fact acting without authority. There is nothing to stop anyone who thinks the Constitution to be worthwhile actually signing it and agreeing with others who are also willing to sign it that they will make laws for each other within its remit, provided that they allow non-signers to live in peace.

It is only fair to conclude this part by noting that a legitimate state governing by consent is not actually impossible. It *is* theoretically possible that three million or ten million or 100 million people could reach and maintain a consensus on all social and political matters without ever diverging. I hope I will not be accused of excessive negativity if I suggest that such a possibility is just a tiny bit unlikely unless the invasion of the body snatchers had actually been successful and we just did not notice. If such consensus is practically unattainable, it is hard to disagree with A. John Simmons when he says '. . . modern

liberal democratic governments do not enjoy the consent of the
governed. . . . Perhaps consent theory tells the whole story about
political obligations and authority. If so, however, it is a very short story,
with philosophical anarchism as its (for some, unhappy) ending'. It
may be an unhappy ending for those who are still prey to the illusions
regarding the legitimacy of representative democracies – it is not an
unhappy ending for me.[47]

Constitutions are not contracts

Of course, some would dispute Spooner's presumption that the
Constitution, to have legal effect, must be construed as a contract.
Perhaps it is not a contract but is nonetheless binding and thus
authoritative.

Edmund Burke offers us a different account of the foundations of
political order, one that is, in essence, non-contractual. His account
begins, perhaps perversely, with the claim that 'Society is indeed a
contract' which might seem to undermine my statement that his
account is non-contractual, but Burke's idea of the social contract is
a very special one. Ordinary contracts, what Burke calls 'subordinate
contracts for objects of mere occasional interest' concern themselves
with such low matters as a 'partnership agreement in a trade of pepper
and coffee, calico, or tobacco' but the contract that concerns the
very foundation of the state is not of this order. This contract that has
now inexplicably become a partnership 'is to be looked on with other
reverence, because it is not a partnership in things subservient only to
the gross animal existence of a temporary and perishable nature'. No.
There is nothing mundane about this partnership that is 'a partnership
in all science; a partnership in all art; a partnership in every virtue and in
all perfection'.[48] And because the objects of this contract or partnership
cannot, it seems, be achieved immediately, or even in a few generations,
it turns out to subsist not only between one living being and another
but also between the living, the dead and the unborn.

It seems that this political partnership (which has once again been re-termed a contract) is a species of transcendent entity, of which particular political partnerships are mere local habitations: 'Each contract of each particular state is but a clause in the great primeval contract of eternal society, linking the lower with the higher natures, connecting the visible and invisible world, according to a fixed compact sanctioned by the inviolable oath which holds all physical and all moral natures, each in their appointed place.'[49]

The primeval and eternal partnership or contract (now become a compact) is, it appears, sanctioned by an inviolable oath, though what the wording of this oath is, who takes it and when it has been or is to be taken, is mysteriously left unspecified. This partnership or contract or compact has the further interesting characteristic that it is 'not subject to the will of those who by an obligation above them, and infinitely superior, are bound to submit their will to that law'. The eternal and primeval contract or partnership or compact or law (it has now become a law) demands the submission of our wills. One may not, except under some kind of (unspecified) necessity that is not chosen but rather thrust upon one, refuse to submit to this contract or partnership or compact or law:

> The municipal corporations of that universal kingdom are not morally at liberty at their pleasure, and on their speculations of a contingent improvement, wholly to separate and tear asunder the bands of their subordinate community and to dissolve it into an unsocial, uncivil, unconnected chaos of elementary principles. It is the first and supreme necessity only, a necessity that is not chosen but chooses, a necessity paramount to deliberation, that admits no discussion and demands no evidence, which alone can justify a resort to anarchy.[50]

A voluntary and rational rejection of the transcendent, eternal and primeval contract or partnership or compact or law would, according to Burke, have devastating consequences. That way, it seems, madness lies, for if we were to choose to make what is in reality a matter of necessity a matter of choice 'the law is broken, nature is disobeyed, and the rebellious are outlawed, cast forth, and exiled from this world of reason, and order, and peace, and virtue, and fruitful penitence, into the antagonist world of madness, discord, vice, confusion, and unavailing sorrow'.[51]

It is interesting to note that, some fifteen years before he wrote these words, Burke was somewhat less pessimistic about the consequences of a rejection of the transcendent political order on which he was to wax so eloquent: 'A new, strange, unexpected face of things appeared. Anarchy is found tolerable. A vast province has now subsisted, and subsisted in a considerable degree of health and vigour, for near a twelvemonth, without governor, without public council, without judges, without executive magistrates.'[52]

It is hard not to be carried away on the floodtide of Burke's eloquence, an eloquence honed, no doubt, in Trinity College's debating society in a tradition not yet atrophied. To appreciate the passage properly requires it to be read as a unit and not piecemeal as I have presented it. Some struggle to° swim against the tide. Frank Turner remarks, 'An unrestrained passion infuses his pages and drives his argument, while an ornate, distant, unfamiliar rhetoric interferes with the persuasiveness of his presentation – in fact, it almost blocks our access to it. Burke's pulsating emotion and the rhetorical vehemence of his assault on the political violence in France press the reader to take refuge in the very rationality he denounces.'[53] On the other hand, Conor Cruise O'Brien plays down the criticism of rhetorical excess: 'There is, in reality, very little rhetoric, quantitatively speaking . . . Most of the book . . . is made up of plain, cogent argument.'[54]

Whatever the merits of the claim and counter-claim in the context of Burke's *Essay* as a whole, the passage just considered is not a page from a novel nor yet a stanza of a poem nor a leader in *The Daily Telegraph* but is, one presumes, a serious and rational attempt to reject mundane contractarianism as the root of the legitimacy of the political order. Shorn of its rhetoric, however, it appears to be (*pace* O'Brien) entirely devoid of argument, amounting to a bare assertion that there is a great primeval eternal contract (in Burke's very special sense of that term) that demands our obedience. Where this contract came from, what its terms are, precisely why we are bound by it – none of these issues is explicitly articulated. Nor is it easy to see how Burke reconciles such sentiments with his commitment to Whiggery with its apotheosis of the so-called Glorious Revolution of 1688 which, ironically, justified itself by charging James II with breaking the original contract between king and people![55] The best that can be said for this passage is that it contains a tacit, pragmatic appeal to much the same fear that one finds at the root of Hobbes's *Leviathan*, namely, that without the state chaos ensues. There is a deep irony in this, given that it would be harder to find two thinkers more diametrically opposed to one other than Burke and Hobbes and that 'What Burke deplored in his particular characterization of the policies of the new French Government was their embodiment of the absolutist state about which Hobbes had theorized.'[56]

If the fundamental political order is not a function of contract, understood in the ordinary, mundane, non-Burkean sense of that term, is Burke's 'grand primeval contract' then to be understood as a function of status? The *locus classicus* for the distinction between relations predicated upon status and upon contract is Sir Henry Maine's *Ancient Law*. There he writes:

> All the forms of *Status* taken notice of in the Law of Persons were derived from, and to some extent are still coloured by, the powers and privileges anciently residing in the Family. If then we employ *Status*, agreeably with the usage of the best writers, to signify these personal conditions only, and avoid applying the term to such conditions as are the immediate or remote result of agreement, we may say that the movement of the progressive societies has hitherto been a movement *from Status to Contract*.[57]

Of course there are status relationships operative in our lives that are simply given to us and are not a matter of choice. The primary locus of such a status relationship is the family but it is a fundamental mistake, a mistake repeatedly attempted, to portray the ideal political order as a family writ large. In Confucian thought, for example, politics is explicitly conceived of in terms of an extension of family relations from the natural family to society at large and one does not have to travel all the way to China to find other instances of the same. But political relations are not family relations writ large, not, that is, unless you want to return to the age of peonage and serfdom. The problem with Burke's position, then, is that if it is to have any plausibility at all, it can have such only by confusing the civil order with its multifarious forms of status relationships with the political order.

And if political relations are not family relations writ large, neither can they be constructed on organic models. We are all familiar (from Plato, St Paul and others) with efforts to understand the political order in biological terms so that we may speak of the 'body politic' and, within that metaphor, attempt to elucidate political relations in terms of the relationships of body parts to each other. It is easy enough to see that the 'body politic' is a figure of speech and not something to be taken literally. It is, perhaps, more difficult to resist the identification of the civil and the political orders, since both are forms of social organization. But status relationships are one thing, contractual relationships quite another. There have been times when the two may have run the risk of being conflated as, for example, in the Catholic conception of marriage which regards it as a status relationship that is nonetheless entered via contract. (For an orthodox Catholic, to speak of 'my ex-wife' is as linguistically odd as it would be to speak of 'my ex-brother') However, such a conception of status-via-contract does not, in the end, conflate the two conditions but simply makes one the condition of entry upon another.

So, then, for Spooner, constitutions purport, but fail, to be contracts; for Burke, they are instantiations of something much grander, lying beyond the reach of human choice, more a matter of status than any ordinary mundane contract could possibly be. If status and contract are the only two possibilities that can ground the legitimacy of the fundamental political order – and it is difficult to see what other possibilities there can be – and if neither of these is tenable, then constitutions are groundless and without authority.

Of the three possibilities considered – that a constitution is an explicit contract, an implicit contract or not a contract at all – I would argue that only the third possibility is in any way plausible. If the contract story in both its varieties is a fiction, as I believe it is, and if one rejects as groundless the Burkean metaphysics, as I believe one must, then unless there is some other theoretical possibility not yet canvassed that will supply us with a rationally defensible foundation for constitutions one is left with constitutions of no authority.

In summary, if the democratic state is not legitimized by being representative, and if constitutions have no authority, where then does the legitimacy of the modern state reside? I suspect the answer might be that, like the smile of the Cheshire cat, it is suspended in mid-air, devoid of any substantial support.

7
CONCLUSION

What I have tried to do in this book is to make the case for libertarian anarchy and for the illegitimacy of the modern state – two sides of the same coin. If what we do and what we are as human beings is to mean anything, we must be free to make our choices and live with their consequences. Unless we are psychopaths, our ability to act freely is not and cannot be completely unlimited but I have argued that it should be limited only by the requirement that we do not infringe on the like freedom of others. The non-aggression principle (NAP) expresses this requirement and, though there may be disputes as to whether a particular action is or is not an instance of aggression, what the NAP demands of us is reasonably obvious in practical terms most of the time. By distinguishing sharply between the requirements of justice based on the NAP and the wider and deeper moral responsibilities that we have towards others, I have tried to show that it is a mistake (a mistake made by J. S. Mill and, to a certain extent, by Hayek) to conflate the notion of aggression with the more amorphous notion of harm. Libertarianism puts no limit on the moral obligations that we choose to recognize, but apart from obvious areas of overlap between morality and justice such as homicide, theft and the like, it utterly rejects the idea that morality as such should be given legal effect.

Underlying the non-aggression principle is the more basic principle of reciprocity. The appeal of this principle is intuitive and can be rejected only by a spectacularly implausible form of special pleading ('I'm so special, so brilliant, so charming, so ethically superior that I cannot be expected to be restrained by the limitations that apply to my inferiors'). However, if someone wants to reject the principle of reciprocity and is prepared to live with the consequences of that rejection I have nothing further to add in argument except to appeal to them to be serious. If they do not want to conform their beliefs to their practices, then at least they could try to conform their practices to their beliefs. As Aristotle pointed out a long time ago in his *Nicomachean Ethics*, it is futile to try to demonstrate the indemonstrable; in any case, in ethics and politics we cannot achieve the kind of certainty that may be attainable in other areas of human enquiry: 'we must be satisfied to indicate the truth with a rough and general sketch: when the subject and the basis of a discussion consist of matters that hold good only as a general rule, but not always, the conclusions reached must be of the same order'.[1]

When plotted on the left–right continuum using the standard, if inadequate, tool of political analysis, libertarianism is perhaps most often bracketed with conservatism. It is much less often associated with liberalism although they would have much in common in their rejection of many state restrictions on personal freedom. I have tried to show the inadequacies of the left–right continuum as a tool of analysis, arguing that libertarianism cuts across that continuum, and by indicating those areas in which libertarianism and conservatism and libertarianism and liberalism coincide and those in which they do not.

The only mode of social organization that is ethically acceptable is one that respects our liberty, namely, anarchy. Perhaps it may be worthwhile to point out one last time that anarchy is not chaos or disorder or mayhem but the spontaneous order that arises from free and mutually acceptable human interactions. Most human beings for most of human history have lived in a state of anarchy; most of our daily interaction with our family, friends, neighbours and colleagues is framed by anarchy, and anarchy is the only mode of organization that is consistent with our accepting responsibility for ourselves, our families and our communities in an adult way.

An issue that divides anarchists is whether or not anyone has the right to the exclusive ownership of natural resources. I have sketched an account of property and property acquisition that disputes the claims of libertarians and anarchists of a socialist or communitarian persuasion that owners of private property are, as it were, tenants who owe a rent to their landlords, the whole human race. If such claims could be substantiated, taxation (and very likely a state to do the taxing) is well on the way to being justified. In addition to dealing with this vitally important topic I have also tried to give expression to some of the more common objections to anarchy and to indicate, as least in a preliminary way, how they might be met.

There are many ways to interfere with a person's liberty but the most spectacular and successful mode of such interference in all of human history is the state. In Chapter 2, I gave a brief account of the bloody and violent history of the state's origins and tried to show how taxation and war go hand in hand. I argued for the presumptive application of ordinary moral standards to the actions of the state and its agents in contrast to the widespread assumption that 'reasons of state' justify the state doing things that are prohibited to ordinary mortals

The central objection to anarchy is that it cannot meet the need for law, order and justice. In Chapter 5, I tried to show that customary law is covalent with society, that it arises from the context of dispute resolution, that it focuses (primarily) on core matters of justice and that we can see a similarity and convergence among the customary laws of societies widely divergent in space and time. A brief discussion of some quasi-anarchic societies reveals the kind of principles upon which a contemporary anarchic society could be constructed, provided we leave behind their historically conditioned deformities. Such principles might include the following: individual rights and private property would take centre stage; victims of crime or their agents would be the primary enforcers of the law; violence would be avoided by the emergence of standard mutually agreeable adjudicative procedures; restitution or reparation (primarily but not exclusively economic) would follow from treating offences as torts (invasions of personal rights) rather than crimes (offences against the state); the enforcement mechanism would be ostracism, blackballing, blacklisting, banishment or exclusion from society and legal change would come about by evolution rather than by (legislative) revolution. In a libertarian legal code, custom and traditional practice could not be the ultimate criteria of what the law would be. Any such law code would have to be based on the principle of non-aggression, with elaborated principles of property rights and rules of evidence. Furthermore, kinship is unlikely to play a hugely significant role in any set of modern legal structures, but since the primary function of kinship in customary legal orders was to provide sureties that function can easily be taken over by insurance companies.

The claim to legitimacy of the modern state rests largely on its democratic credentials. In Chapter 6, I challenged the idea that representative democracy erases the distinction between ruler and ruled and so justifies the democratic state. I did this by calling into question the idea that there can be such a thing as political representation. Another potent source for the legitimacy of the modern state is the idea that it is justified because it rests on a constitutional basis. Once again, I have tried to show that constitutions as such have no special authority and, in particular, cannot justify the coercive actions of some against others in a society who have made no explicit commitment to its terms.

NOTES

Chapter 1: Introduction

1 See Craig Duncan and Tibor Machan (2005), *Libertarianism: For and Against* (Lanham, MD: Rowman and Littlefield), p. 46ff.

2 Ibid., p. 46.

3 Ibid., p. 47.

4 Murray N. Rothbard (2002 [1982]), *The Ethics of Liberty* (New York: New York University Press), p. 166.

5 H. L. Mencken (1982), *A Mencken Chrestomathy* (New York: Vintage Books), p. 147.

6 Jan Narveson (2008), *You and the State: A Fairly Brief Introduction to Political Philosophy* (Lanham, MD: Rowman and Littlefield), p. 1.

7 See Ralph Raico (2006), 'Classical Liberal Roots of the Marxist Doctrine of Classes', available at http://mises.org/daily/2217.

8 See Sheldon Richman (2011), 'Libertarian Left', *The American Conservative*, available at www.amconmag.com/blog/libertarian-left/.

9 See Narveson (2008), p. 183.

10 Material of a somewhat more practical bent from a variety of libertarian perspectives can be found in David Boaz (1997), *The Libertarian Reader* (New York: The Free Press); Randall Fitzgerald (2003), *Mugged By the State: Outrageous Government Assaults on Ordinary People and their Property* (Washington, DC: Regnery Publishing); David Friedman (1989), *The Machinery of Freedom: A Guide to a Radical Capitalism* (La Salle, IL: Open Court); Robert Higgs (2004), *Against Leviathan: Government Power and a Free Society* (Oakland, CA: Independent Institute); Jacob H. Huebert (2010), *Libertarianism Today* (Oxford: Praeger); Jeffrey A. Miron (2010), *Libertarianism, from A to Z* (New York: Basic Books); Charles

Murray (1992), *What It Means to be a Libertarian* (New York: Broadway); and Murray N. Rothbard (2006), *For a New Liberty*, 2nd edn (Auburn, AL: Ludwig von Mises Institute).

11 See Alfred G. Cuzan (1979), 'Do We Ever Really get out of Anarchy?', *The Journal of Libertarian Studies*, 3 (2), 151–8 and (2010), 'Revisiting "Do We Ever Really get out of Anarchy?"', *The Journal of Libertarian Studies*, 22, 3–21.

Chapter 2: Death and taxes

1 Charles Tilly (1985), 'War Making and State Making as Organized Crime', in Peter Evans, Dietrich Rueschemeyer and Theda Skocpol (eds), *Bringing the State Back In* (Cambridge: Cambridge University Press), 169–87, p. 170.

2 Charles Tilly (1992 [1990]), *Coercion, Capital and European States, AD 990–1992*, revised edn (Oxford: Blackwell), p. 1; p. 43.

3 Robert C. Ellickson (1991), *Order without Law: How Neighbors Settle Disputes* (Cambridge, MA: Harvard University Press), pp. 127–8.

4 Max Weber (1919), *Politik als Beruf (Politics as a Vocation)* (Munich: Duncker & Humboldt).

5 Ibid.

6 Murray N. Rothbard (2002 [1982]), *The Ethics of Liberty* (New York: New York University Press), p. 172.

7 A government is 'a group of people who claim and, to an effective extent, exercise a monopoly of coercion resting on deadly force over a definite geographical area, and the artifacts and procedures by which they do so'. Crispin Sartwell (2008), *Against the State* (Albany, NY: State University of New York Press), p. 27. See also Gianfranco Poggi (1990), *The State: Its Nature, Development and Prospects* (Cambridge: Polity Press).

8 Bruce A. Ackerman (1980), *Social Justice in the Liberal State* (New Haven, CT: Yale University Press), p. 252 n. 8.

9 R. G. Collingwood (1940), *Metaphysics* (Oxford: Clarendon Press).

10 Ludwig Wittgenstein (1969), *On Certainty*, G. E. M. Anscombe and G. H von Wright (eds), trans. Denis Paul and G. E. M. Anscombe (Oxford: Blackwell), passim.

11 James C. Scott (2009), *The Art of Not Being Governed* (New Haven, CT: Yale University Press), p. 3.

12 Immanuel Kant (1963 [1786]), 'The Conjectural Beginnings of Human History', in Lewis White Beck (ed.), *Kant: On History* (New York: Bobbs-Merrill), pp. 53–68.

13 Adam Smith (1978 [1762/1766]), *Lectures on Jurisprudence*, R. L. Meek, D. D. Raphael and P. G. Stein (eds) (Oxford: Oxford University Press), p. 14. [A 1, 27].

14 'The founding of agrarian states, then, was the contingent event that created a distinction, hence a dialectic, between a settled, state-governed population and a frontier penumbra of less governed or virtually autonomous peoples.' Scott (2009), pp. 3–4.

15 As the title of the long-running BBC series has it, 'Only Fools and Horses' work. Incidentally, the hero – perhaps central character might be a better description – of that series Del Boy Trotter is a proto-anarchist who says, 'The government don't give us nothing, so we don't give the government nothing.'

16 Franz Oppenheimer (1975 [1919]), *The State*, trans. John Gitterman (New York: Free Life Editions), chapter 2a.

17 Thomas Hobbes (1996 [1651]), *Leviathan* (Cambridge: Cambridge University Press), p. 118.

18 'One could see . . . why the hunting tribes and primitive peasants never formed a State. Primitive peasants never made enough of an economic accumulation to be worth stealing . . .' Albert J. Nock (1928), *On Doing the Right Thing* (New York: Harper & Brothers), p. 151.

19 Mancur Olson (1993), 'Dictatorship, Democracy, and Development', *American Political Science Review*, 87 (9), 567–76.

20 Oppenheimer (1975 [1919]), p. 13. 'The State originated in conquest and confiscation, as a device for maintaining the stratification of society permanently into two classes – an owning and exploiting class, relatively small, and a propertyless dependent class. . . . No State known to history originated in any other manner, or for any other purpose than to enable the continuous economic exploitation of one class by another.' Nock (1928), p. 150.

21 David Hume (1826 [1748]), 'Of the Original Contract', in T. H. Green and T. H. Grose (eds), *Essays Moral, Political, and Literary* (London: Longmans and Green), p. 515.

22 Anthony de Jasay (1997), *Against Politics: On Government, Anarchy and Order* (London: Routledge), p. 36.

23 Crispin Sartwell (2008), *Against the State* (Albany, NY: State University of New York Press), p. 39.

24 Clarence S. Darrow (2011 [1903]), *Resist Not Evil* (Auburn, AL: Ludwig von Mises Institute), p. 3.

25 Ibid.

26 See Tilly (1992 [1990]), p. 1.

27 Scott (2009), p. 7.

28 Harold J. Berman (1983), *Law and Revolution* (Cambridge, MA: Harvard University Press), passim.

29 Tilly (1992 [1990]), p. 43. The question that Tilly thinks must be answered is: 'What accounts for the great variation over time and space in the kind of states that have prevailed in Europe since AD 990 and why did European states eventually converge on difference variants of the nation state?' (p. 5). He locates the primary determinants of our modern state system in two phenomena: capital and coercion. Capital he regards as 'any tangible mobile resources, and enforceable claims on such resources' (p. 17). While coercion is defined as 'all concerted application, threatened or actual, of action that commonly causes loss or damage to the persons or possession of individuals or groups who are aware of both the action and the potential damage' (p. 19).

30 Edward Ames and Richard T. Rapp (1977), 'The Birth and Death of Taxes: A Hypothesis', *Journal of Economic History*, 37 (1), 161–78, p. 164.

31 Ibid., p. 170.

32 Fukuyama writes: 'One of the Glorious Revolution's main accomplishments was to make taxation legitimate because it was henceforth clearly based on consent.' Francis Fukuyama (2011), *The Origins of Political Order* (London: Profile Books), p. 419. Not quite. What it actually did was to eliminate the distinction between the executive power demanding taxes and the body supposed to represent the taxpayers.

33 Ames and Rapp (1977), p. 170; p. 174.

34 Fukuyama (2011), p. 330.

35 de Jasay (1997), p. 86.

36 Olwen Hufton (1994), *Europe: Privilege and Protest 1730–1789* (London: Fontana Press), p. 95.

37   'In no Protestant country did the Church provide a truly effective obstacle
to state control. In the main its authority and privileges were not such as
to incur the opposition of secular powers nor did it feel the uncomfortable
blast of the impious Enlightenment except perhaps in Scotland.' Hufton
(1994), p. 58.

38   'Towns everywhere housed bureaucrats, great and small, who existed
above all to tax, to police and to regulate society.' Hufton (1994), p. 40.

39   See Berman (1983), passim.

40   See Fukuyama (2011), passim.

41   Tilly (1992 [1990]), pp. 2–3. In using the term national state he does *not*
mean what we would today call a nation-state, a state whose inhabitants
share an identity along linguistic, religious and symbolic lines.

42   Ibid.

43   Thomas Ertman (1997), *Birth of the Leviathan: Building States and
Regimes in Medieval and Early Modern Europe* (Cambridge: Cambridge
University Press), p. 1.

44   Tilly (1992 [1990]), p. 43.

45   See Hufton (1994), p. 67. 'In central Europe a concept of the state was
weakest of all and the ramifications of power within the 294 states of the
German Empire almost impossible to define.' Hufton (1994), p. 68.

46   Tilly (1985), p. 171.

47   Tilly (1985), p. 170. See de Jasay (1997), p. 16. Where he argues that the
origin of the state in conquest and its origin in social contract are not rival
explanations.

48   Rothbard (2006), p. 56.

49   Frank van Dun (2006), 'What is Kritarchy?', in Michael van Notten (2006),
*The Law of the Somalis: A Stable Foundation for Economic Development
in the Horn of Africa* (Trenton, NJ: Red Sea Press), p. 193.

50   See Carkuff (2010).

51   van Dun (2006), p. 193.

52   Some material in the following paragraphs first appeared in Casey
(2007).

53   Rothbard (2006), pp. 56–7.

54   Rothbard (2006), p. 56.

55   Albert J. Nock (1928), *On Doing the Right Thing* (New York: Harper
Brothers Publishers).

56 Mencken (1982 [1916]), pp. 148–9.

57 de Jasay (1997), p. 76. Emphasis added. Fukuyama defines legitimacy as meaning that 'the people who make up the society recognize the fundamental justice of the system as a whole and are willing to abide by its rules'. Fukuyama (2011), p. 42.

58 There is an amusing irony in the failure of those who vehemently deny the possibility of anarchic individual relationships to recognize that we currently have an anarchic system fully operational in the sphere of international relations. 'In the existing world, each land area is ruled over by a State organization, with a number of States scattered over the earth, each with a monopoly of violence over its own territory. No super-State exists with a monopoly of violence over the entire world; and so a state of "anarchy" exists between the several States.' Rothbard (2002), pp. 191–2.

59 Rothbard (2002), p. 169.

60 See Wittgenstein (1969), pp. 117–19.

61 Murray Rothbard (1973), 'A Future of Peace and Capitalism', in James H. Weaver (ed.), *Modern Political Economy* (Boston: Allyn and Bacon).

62 de Jasay (1997), p. 77.

63 Sartwell (2008), p. 41.

64 Bertrand de Jouvenal (1955), *Sovereignty: An Inquiry into the Political Good* (Chicago: University of Chicago Press), p. xiii.

65 See de Jasay (1997), p. 2.

66 Rothbard recognizes this as the most difficult task of the libertarian anarchist. 'How could private enterprise and the free market possibly provide such service? How could police, legal systems, judicial services, law enforcement, prisons – how could these be provided in a free market?' Rothbard (2006), p. 267.

67 This is what Aeon Skoble calls, the 'Hobbesian Fear.' See Aeon J. Skoble (2008b), *Deleting the State: An Argument about Government* (Chicago: Open Court), chapter 3.

68 While the findings of Game Theory are not uncontroversial, the general indication is that it is rational (as well as moral), to avoid predation in long-run interactions. This reflects the common-sense notion that it is not a good idea to cheat, steal from or lie to someone you're going to have to work with or do business with again.

69 See M. White (2011a), 'Source List and Detailed Death Tolls for Man-Made Multicides throughout History', available at http://necrometrics.com/

warstats.htm, and M. White (2011b), 'Death by Mass Unpleasantness: Estimated Totals for the Entire 20th Century', available at http://users. erols.com/mwhite28/warstat8.htm.

70   See on this point Alfred G. Cuzan, (1979), 'Do We Ever Really Get Out of Anarchy?', *The Journal of Libertarian Studies*, 3 (2), pp. 151–58.

71   Scott (1998), p. 3. Scott is anxious to make clear that he is not an anarchist. 'The state, as I make abundantly clear, is the vexed institution that is the ground of both our freedoms and our unfreedoms.' Scott (1998), p. 7. But the whole tenor of Scott's thought moves him inexorably in the anarchist direction. He appears to be repelled by the unpalatable results of what he regards as the unfettered market coordination proceeding from the thought of Hayek and Friedman but he would seem to be confusing the free market with the present state-sponsored system of mercantilist capitalism that is as much anathema to free marketeers as it would appear to be to him.

72   From Kropotkin's 'On Anarchism' in Robert Graham, (ed.) (2005), *Anarchism: A Documentary History of Libertarian Ideas: Volume One: From Anarchy to Anarchism (300CE to 1939)* (London: Black Rose Books).

73   Rothbard (2002), p. 187.

74   Ibid.

Chapter 3: Liberty and libertarianism

1   Barry Deutsch (2011), 'The 24 Types of Libertarian', available at www. leftycartoons.com/the-24-types-of-libertarian/. See also Christopher Beam (2011), 'The Trouble with Liberty', *New York* available at http:// nymag.com/news/politics/70282/; Jeff Riggenbach (2011b), 'The Ignorance of New York Magazine', available at http://mises.org/daily/4990/ The-Ignorance-of-iNew-Yorki-Magazine and Robert P. Murphy (2011b), 'Christopher Beam Takes On Libertarianism', available at http://mises. org/daily/4956.

2   See Jeff Riggenbach (2011b), 'The Ignorance of New York Magazine', available at http://mises.org/daily/4990/The-Ignorance-of-iNew-Yorki-Magazine.

3   Justin Raimondo (2000), *Enemy of the State* (Amherst, NY: Prometheus Books), p. 214.

4 In the discussion that follows, I am, unless specifically stated otherwise, dealing with competent adult human beings. Non-competent adult human beings and children require special consideration.

5 Osterfeld, David (2007), 'Freedom, Society, and the State: An Investigation Into the Possibility of Society without Government (excerpt)', in Edward Stringham (ed.), (2007), *Anarchy and the Law: The Political Economy of Choice* (New Brunswick: Transaction), p. 504.

6 George Washington (1796), 'The Address of General Washington to The People of The United States on his Declining of the Presidency of the United States', *American Daily Advertiser*.

7 Doug Carkuff (2010), 'Libertarianism is Kidstuff', available at www.ncc-1776.org/tle2010/tle556–20100207-05.html.

8 Stephan Kinsella (2011), 'What Libertarianism Is', available at http://mises.org/daily/3660.

9 Crispin Sartwell (2008), *Against the State* (Albany, NY: State University of New York Press), p. 48.

10 Peter Vallentyne (2010), 'Libertarianism', in Edward N. Zalta (ed.), *The Stanford Encyclopedia of Philosophy*. Vallentyne draws a distinction between this self-ownership account of libertarianism and what he calls 'Spencerian' Libertarianism which is the position that 'each agent has a right to maximum equal empirical negative liberty'. Some take the two positions to be functionally equivalent while others take them to be at best only partially coincident.

11 See Sheldon Richman (2011), 'Libertarian Left', available at www.amconmag.com/blog/libertarian-left/.

12 See James Peron (2001), 'Are There Two Libertarianisms?', *Freeman*, 51 (6), pp. 39–42.

13 Murray N. Rothbard (2002 [1982]), *The Ethics of Liberty* (New York: New York University Press), p. 24.

14 Sartwell (2008), p. 21.

15 Ibid. p. 103.

16 See David Schmidtz (2006), *Elements of Justice* (Cambridge: Cambridge University Press), pp. 73–103.

17 Cicero (1998), *The Republic and The Laws*, trans. Niall Rudd (Oxford University Press), p. 9 [I, 21].

18 See Aeon J. Skoble (2008b), *Deleting the State: An Argument about Government* (Chicago: Open Court), p. 23ff.

19 Sartwell (2008), p. 54.

20 Aschwin de Wolf notes that 'De Jasay considers his work on the presumption of liberty a central component of his oeuvre. I think that the argument is most persuasive in conveying to classical liberals and libertarians the message to abandon their tortured attempts to provide a justificationist framework in defence of liberty.' Aschwin de Wolf (2011), 'Review of de Jasay's Political Philosophy, Clearly', *Economic Affairs*, 31 (2), p. 197.

21 See Anthony de Jasay (2010b), 'Freedom, from a Mainly Logical Perspective', in Anthony de Jasay (2010a), *Political Philosophy, Clearly: Essays on Freedom and Fairness, Property and Equalities* (Indianapolis: The Liberty Fund), pp. 206–27.

22 Sartwell (2008), pp. 18–19.

23 Walter E. Block (2008 [1976]), *Defending the Undefendable* (Auburn, AL: Ludwig von Mises Institute), pp. 41–6.

24 John Stuart Mill (1974), *On Liberty* (London: Penguin), p. 164.

25 Some of the following appears in Casey (2012), 'The Inescapability of Ethics', forthcoming in F. O'Rourke *What Happened in and to Moral Philosophy in the Twentieth Century?: Philosophical Essays in Honour of Alisdair Macintyre*. Notre Dame, Indiana: The University of Notre Dame Press.

26 Iris Murdoch (1994), *Metaphysics as a Guide to Morals* (London: Penguin), p. 203.

27 Charles Darwin (1881 [1897]), 'Letter to William Graham, 3 July 1881', in Francis Darwin (ed.), *The Life and Letters of Charles Darwin*, 3 vols (London: John Murray).

28 Lynne Rudder Baker (1987), *Saving Belief: A Critique of Physicalism* (Princeton, NJ: Princeton University Press), p. 134.

29 Some of the material in the following section first appeared in Casey (2011).

30 Adapted from Jacob G. Hornberger (2011), 'Conservatism vs. Libertarianism', available at www.fff.org/comment/com0604c.asp.

31 Russell Kirk (1984), 'Libertarians: The Chirping Sectaries', in G. W. Carey (ed.), *Freedom and Virtue: the Conservative/Libertarian debate* (Lanham, MD: University Press of America), pp. 113–24.

32 Tibor Machan (1984), 'Libertarianism: The Principle of Liberty', in G. W. Carey (ed.), *Freedom and Virtue: the Conservative/Libertarian debate* (Lanham, MD: University Press of America), 35–58, p. 38.

33 Robert Nisbet (1984), 'Conservatives and Libertarians: Uneasy Cousins', in G. W. Carey (ed.), *Freedom and Virtue: the Conservative/Libertarian debate* (Lanham, MD: University Press of America), 13–24, p. 21.

34 Murray N. Rothbard (1984), 'Frank S. Meyer: The Fusionist as Libertarian Manqué', in G. W. Carey (ed.), *Freedom and Virtue: the Conservative/Libertarian debate* (Lanham, MD: University Press of America), 91–111, p. 95.

35 Machan (1984), p. 39.

36 Rothbard (1984), p. 92.

37 Machan (1984), pp. 46–7.

38 Ibid., p. 49.

39 See W. Berns (1984), 'The Need for Public Authority', in G. W. Carey (ed.), *Freedom and Virtue: the Conservative/Libertarian debate* (Lanham, MD: University Press of America), pp. 25–33.

40 Machan (1984), p. 48.

41 Rothbard (2002), p. 24.

42 Ibid.

Chapter 4: Anarchy and anarchism

1 I refer the reader to the following: for a convenient compendium of original writings, see Robert Graham (ed.), (2005), *Anarchism: A Documentary History of Libertarian Ideas: Volume One: From Anarchy to Anarchism (300CE to 1939)* (Montreal and London: Black Rose Books), and Robert Graham (2007), *Anarchism: A Documentary History of Libertarian Ideas: Volume Two: The Anarchist Current (1939–2006)* (Montreal and London: Black Rose Books). For an overview of some particular anarchic thinkers, see Anon (ed.), (2010a), *Anarchist Academics: Noam Chomsky, David D. Friedman, Murray Rothbard, Howard Zinn, Peter Neville, Jan Narveson, Murray Bookchin* (Memphis, TN: Books LLC). For a convenient online survey of anarcho-capitalism, see Hogeye Bill (2011),

'Anarcho-Capitalist FAQ', available at www.ozarkia.net/bill/anarchism/
faq.html. For a somewhat broader perspective but still from within the
perspective of the individual anarchistic tradition, see Bryan Caplan (No
Date), 'Appendix: Defining Anarchism', available at http://econfaculty.
gmu.edu/bcaplan/def.htm and (2011), 'Anarchist Theory FAQ', available
at http://econfaculty.gmu.edu/bcaplan/anarfaq.htm. Finally, for a rich
source of material critical of the pretensions of anarcho-capitalism,
individual anarchism and libertarian anarchism to be genuinely anarchic
see Infoshop.org (1995), 'An Anarchist FAQ', available at www.infoshop.
org/page/AnAnarchistFAQ.

2 Perhaps the best known among the anarchists are Peter Kropotkin,
Michael Bakunin, Pierre-Joseph Proudhon and Max Stirner but, as one
might expect, there are many other thinkers to whom that description
can be attached, ranging from the seventeenth century proto-anarchist
Gerrard Winstanley and the eighteenth century William Godwin to the
latter-day Noam Chomsky and Murray Bookchin.

3 D. Novak (1958), 'The Place of Anarchism in the History of Political
Thought', *The Review of Politics*, 20 (3), 307–29, p. 325.

4 See Caplan (No Date). To see just how tiresome and pointless 'arguments
by definition' can be, see the response to Caplan's piece in Anon (No
Date), 'Replies to some Errors and Distortions in Bryan Caplan's 'Anarchist
Theory FAQ' version 5.2', available at www.spunk.org/texts/intro/faq/
sp001547/append1.html.

5 'I don't know what you mean by "glory"', Alice said. Humpty Dumpty
smiled contemptuously. 'Of course you don't – till I tell you. I meant "there's
a nice knock-down argument for you!" 'But "glory" doesn't mean "a nice
knock-down argument"', Alice objected. 'When *I* use a word', Humpty
Dumpty said, in rather a scornful tone, 'it means just what I choose it to
mean – neither more nor less'. 'The question is', said Alice, 'whether you
can make words mean so many different things'. 'The question is', said
Humpty Dumpty, 'which is to be master – that's all'. Lewis Carroll (1972
[1871]), *Through the Looking Glass* (London: Hart-Davis, MacGibbon),
pp. 80–1.

6 Tom Lane (2011), 'On Anarchism: Noam Chomsky interviewed by Tom
Lane', available at www.chomsky.info/interviews/19961223.htm. Eight
years later, Chomsky was still of the same view: 'Anarchism is a very
broad category; it means a lot of different things to different people.'
Barry Pateman (2005), *Chomsky on Anarchism* (Edinburgh: AK Press),
p. 234.

7 Block describes Rothbard as 'an Austro-libertarian anarchist'. Walter Block (2006), 'Kevin Carson as Dr. Jekyll and Mr. Hyde', *The Journal of Libertarian Studies*, 20 (1), p. 42. I am happy to adopt a shorted form of this name. For more on libertarian anarchism, see Aeon Skoble (2008b), *Deleting the State: An Argument about Government* (Chicago: Open Court), p. 20 and passim. Skoble distinguishes, as I do, between libertarian anarchists on the one hand, and libertarian minimal-statists or minarchists on the other.

8 Tom Lane, (1996), 'On Anarchism: Noam Chomsky Interviewed by Tom Lane', available at www.chomsky.info/interviews/19961223.htm.

9 Murray N. Rothbard (1973), 'A Future of Peace and Capitalism', in James H. Weaver (ed.), *Modern Political Economy* (Boston: Allyn and Bacon), p. 419.

10 David Osterfeld (2007), 'Freedom, Society, and the State: An Investigation Into the Possibility of Society without Government (excerpt)', in Edward Stringham (ed.), (2007), *Anarchy and the Law: The Political Economy of Choice* (New Brunswick: Transaction), pp. 505–6.

11 Ibid., p. 506.

12 E. Walter (2006), 'Kevin Carson as Dr. Jekyll and Mr. Hyde', *The Journal of Libertarian Studies*, 20 (1), 35–46, p. 40. See also Sheldon Richman (2011), 'Libertarian Left', *The American Conservative* available at www.amconmag.com/blog/libertarian-left/.

13 See Long (2008), 'Market Anarchism as Constitutionalism', in Roderick T. Long and T. Machan (eds), *Anarchism/Minarchism: Is Government Part of a Free Country?* (Aldershot, Hampshire: Ashgate Publishing), p. 139 on the ambiguity of the term.

14 John D. Sneed (1977), 'Order without Law: Where will Anarchists keep the Madmen?', *Journal of Libertarian Studies*, 1 (2), 117–24, p. 118.

15 See Peter Vallentyne (2010), 'Libertarianism', in Edward N. Zalta (ed.), *The Stanford Encyclopedia of Philosophy* and Michael Otsuka (2003), *Libertarianism without Inequality* (Oxford: Clarendon Press).

16 E. Adamson Hoebel (1954), *The Law of Primitive Man* (Cambridge, MA: Harvard University Press), p. 58.

17 Anthony de Jasay (2010a), *Political Philosophy, Clearly: Essays on Freedom and Fairness, Property and Equalities*, Hartmut Kliemt (ed.) (Indianapolis: The Liberty Fund), p. 22.

18 Ibid., p. 141.

19 The material in the paragraphs following is based in part on Edward Feser (2005), 'There's No Such Thing as an Unjust Initial Acquisition', *Social Philosophy and Policy*, 22 (1), 56–80.

20 'If a resource is really unowned, no one is harmed by someone taking exclusive possession of it, and there is no call for a proviso safeguarding those who are thus excluded.' Anthony de Jasay (2010a), *Political Philosophy, Clearly: Essays on Freedom and Fairness, Property and Equalities*, Hartmut Kliemt (ed.) (Indianapolis: The Liberty Fund), p. 144.

21 And this is not even to consider the following problem created by common ownership. If we all own everything collectively, then Artemis the hunter, if she is to avoid being taken for a thief, would require the consent of everyone to her acquisition of the deer that she has killed and eaten. No one could acquire or use any resources without the permission of all. Under these conditions, the human race would become extinct with commendable promptitude and the problem of property would disappear.

22 G. A. Cohen (1995), *Self-Ownership, Freedom and Equality* (Cambridge: Cambridge University Press), p. 94.

23 See Linda Tannehill & Morris Tannehill (1970), *The Market for Liberty* (San Francisco: Fox & Wilkes), pp. 57–8.

24 See Carol M. Rose (1985), 'Possession as the Origin of Property', *The University of Chicago Law Review*, 52 (1), 73–88, where she makes the case that a possessor of a given portion of land has an obligation to provide a persistent and unambiguous demarcation of that portion's boundaries.

25 David Schmidtz and Jason Brennan (2010), *A Brief History of Liberty* (Oxford: Wiley-Blackwell), p. 109.

26 M. T. Cicero (1998), *The Republic and The Laws*, trans. Niall Rudd (Oxford: Oxford University Press), I, 21.

27 Tannehill and Tannehill (1970), p. 58.

28 de Jasay (2010a), p. 147.

29 See John Hasnas (2008), 'The Obviousness of Anarchy', in Roderick T. Long and Tibor R. Machan (eds), (2008), *Anarchism/Miniarchism: Is Government Part of a Free Country?* (Aldershot, Hampshire: Ashgate Publishing).

30 'Philosophical anarchists are unable to account for co-operation and community.' John Hoffman (1995), *Beyond the State: An Introductory Critique* (Cambridge: Polity Press), p. 113.

31 Ibid., p. 115.

32 Ibid.

33 '. . . those who postulate a stateless society as an extension of the free market cannot plausible tackle the problem of division and inequality'. Ibid., p. 113.

34 'If the state is organized as a repressive hierarchy with formidable and comprehensive powers, how do you remove it without becoming statist as well?' Ibid., p. 12.

35 Crispin Sartwell (2008), *Against the State* (Albany, NY: State University of New York Press), p. 62.

36 See Ewan McKendrick (ed.), (2009), *Goode on Commercial Law* (London: LexisNexis), pp. 174–6.

37 Hasnas 2008, pp. 113–14.

38 See Harold J. Berman (2003), *Law and Revolution II: The Impact of the Protestant Reformations on the Western Legal Tradition* (Cambridge, MA: Belnap Press).

39 See Hasnas (2008), pp. 116–17.

40 This example is taken from Long (2008).

41 Ibid., p. 127.

42 Clive Emsley (2010), *The Great British Bobby: A History of British Policing from the 18th Century to the Present* (London: Quercus), p. 42.

43 Ibid., p. 46.

44 Ibid., p. 7.

45 Hasnas (2008), pp. 124–5.

Chapter 5: Law without orders

1 From the BBC TV Series *Blackadder Goes Forth*, Part IV Episode 6: *Goodbyeee*.

2 See Michael Buchanan (2011), 'Peers concern at "tsunami" of new legislation', *BBC News UK Politics*, available at www.bbc.co.uk/news/uk-politics-14794400.

3 It won't be hard to detect the influence of Friedrich Hayek and Bruce Benson on what follows. While I have been inspired by the work of both authors, I make no claim that my account is a faithful or accurate representation of their thought.

4 J. H. Baker (2007 [2002]), *An Introduction to English Legal History,* 4th edn (Oxford: Oxford University Press), p. 1.

5 Friedrich A. Hayek (1982), *Law, Legislation and Liberty: A New Statement of the Liberal Principles of Justice and Political Economy* (London: Routledge), p. 72.

6 Although I made an effort in that direction in Gerard Casey (1989), 'Angelic Interiority', *Irish Philosophical Journal*, 6 (1), 82–118.

7 Adam Smith (1976 [1776]), *An Inquiry into the Nature and Causes of the Wealth of Nations*, R. H. Campbell, A. S. Skinner and W. B. Todd (eds), 2 vols (Oxford: Clarendon Press), p. 26. [I, ii, 2].

8 St Thomas Aquinas (1946), *Summa Theologica* (New York: Benziger Brothers), I–II, q. 96, a. 2, c.

9 See Robert C. Ellickson (1991), *Order without Law: How Neighbors Settle Disputes* (Cambridge, MA: Harvard University Press), pp. 127–32.

10 Recent work in game theory has shown that 'responsive cooperation is an effective strategy for maximising self-interest'. Aeon J. Skoble (2008a), 'Radical Freedom and Social Living', in Roderick T. Long and T. Machan (eds), *Anarchism/Minarchism: Is a Government part of a Free Country?* 87–102, p. 95.

11 Mario Puzo (1969), *The Godfather* (London: William Heinemann Ltd), p. 88.

12 Baker (2007), p. 4.

13 Bruce L. Benson (1989), 'Enforcement of Private Property Rights in Primitive Societies', *The Journal of Libertarian Studies*, 9 (1–26), 3. John Hasnas notes that '[V]iolence has high costs and produces unpredictable results, human beings naturally seek peaceful alternatives'. John Hasnas (2008), 'The Obviousness of Anarchy', in Roderick T. Long and Tibor R. Machan (eds), (2008), *Anarchism/Miniarchism: Is Government Part of a Free Country?* (Aldershot, Hampshire: Ashgate Publishing), p. 114.

14 '. . . the maintenance of the social order . . . is the source of law'. H. Grotius (1925 [1646]), *De Jure Belli ac Pacis*, trans. Francis W. Kelsey (Oxford: Clarendon Press), p. 12. For an account of how a modern society might function under the kind of law system adumbrated here, see Bruce L. Benson (1990a), 'Customary Law with Private Means of Resolving Disputes and Dispensing Justice: a Description of a Modern System of Law and Order without State Coercion', *The Journal of Libertarian*

Studies, 9 (2), 25–42 and Bruce L. Benson (1990b), *The Enterprise of Law: Justice without the State* (San Francisco: Pacific Research Institute for Public Policy).

15 Baker (2007), p. 4.

16 See Hasnas (2008), p. 114.

17 See Skoble (2008a), p. 99.

18 For a real-life example of the spontaneous emergence of law, see Terry L. Anderson and P. J. Hill (2004), *The Not So Wild Wild West: Property Rights on the Frontier* (Stanford, CA: Stanford University Press).

19 My account is able to provide for what Hart has called 'secondary rules' though without the positivist emphasis that Hart gives to his secondary rules. See H. L. A. Hart (1994 [1961]), *The Concept of Law*, 2nd edn (Oxford: The Clarendon Press), pp. 89–96. Cf. Lon L. Fuller (1964), *The Morality of Law* (New Haven, CT: Yale University Press), passim. See also Bruce L. Benson (1989), 'Enforcement of Private Property Rights in Primitive Societies', *The Journal of Libertarian Studies*, 9 (1–26), 4–6.

20 Only adjudications concerned with assertions of rights will give rise to law. See Lon Fuller (1978), 'The Form and Limits of Adjudication', *Harvard Law Review*, 92 (2), p. 353.

21 The claim that one knows something only if one can give the reason for it is false. I can know that some act is just or unjust without being able to give an account of justice or injustice. Philosophically sophisticated readers will realize that in saying this, I am denying the presupposition of Socrates, in Plato's early dialogues, that knowledge to be knowledge requires the ability to justify what it is that one claims to know.

22 Hasnas (2008), p. 119.

23 Benson includes under spontaneously self-organizing structures 'trading systems and markets, religious systems and congregations, extended family systems, clans, villages, cities, transportation routes *and* customary law'. Bruce Benson (1990a), 'Customary Law with Private Means of Resolving Disputes and Dispensing Justice: A Description of a Modern System of Law and Order without State Coercion', *The Journal of Libertarian Studies*, 9 (2), p. 27.

24 'The basis of Roman law, as of any law, was customary'. A. M. Pritchard (1961), *Leage's Roman Private Law*, 3rd edn (London: Macmillan & Co. Ltd), p. 14.

25 James Coolidge Carter (1907), *Law: Its Origin, Growth and Function* (New York: G. P. Putnam's Sons), pp. 133–4.

26 Randy E. Barnett (1998), *The Structure of Liberty: Justice and the Rule of Law* (Oxford: Oxford University Press), p. 127.

27 Benson (1989), p. 6.

28 Harold J. Berman (1983), *Law and Revolution* (Cambridge, MA: Harvard University Press), p. 55.

29 Murray N. Rothbard (2002 [1982]), *The Ethics of Liberty* (New York: New York University Press), p. 178.

30 Ibid.; see Berman (1983), passim.

31 Ellickson (1991), p. 147.

32 See Gerard Casey (2003), 'Ethics and Human Nature', *American Catholic Philosophical Quarterly*, 77 (4), 519–31.

33 Sextus Aelius was a distinguished jurisconsult of an earlier time.

34 The oft-cited passage from Cicero is *not* found in the extant text of *de re Publica* but is found as a quotation in Lactantius's *Divinae Institutiones*. Lactantius was an early Christian and an admirer or Cicero. The passage is usually placed in book 3 of *de re Publica*.

35 Frank van Dun (2001), 'Natural Law, Liberalism, and Christianity', *The Journal of Libertarian Studies*, 15 (3), 1–36, p. 3.

36 Ibid., 3.

37 Lon L. Fuller (1964), *The Morality of Law* (New Haven, CT: Yale University Press), p. 96.

38 People could be permitted to drive anywhere on a road if, for instance, they agreed not to drive above a walking pace as was the case, more or less, in the early twentieth century.

39 See A. John Simmons (1993), *On the Edge of Anarchy: Locke, Consent, and the Limits of Society* (Princeton, NJ: Princeton University Press), pp. 264–6.

40 Of course, legislation can also concern itself with regulatory matters (which have the form of commands), or permissive matters (which do not have the form of commands), but I am focusing on the essential difference in kind between legislation and customary law and so, for the sake of simplicity, I'll ignore these points.

41 Francis Fukuyama (2011), *The Origins of Political Order* (London: Profile Books), p. 15.

42   See Roy Halliday (2011), 'Historical Examples of Anarchy without Chaos', available at http://royhalliday.home.mindspring.com/history.htm.

43   E. Adamson Hoebel (1954), *The Law of Primitive Man* (Cambridge, MA: Harvard University Press), p. 83.

44   Some believe that the term 'Eskimo' may be offensive to the people it is meant to designate and that the term 'Inuit' should be used instead. Whatever the facts of the matters here, 'Eskimo' is the term used by Hoebel, on whose writings my account is based so for the sake of simplicity I shall continue to employ it throughout the following section.

45   Ibid., p. 67.

46   Ibid., p. 80.

47   Ibid., p. 99.

48   Joseph Peden published his ground-breaking article on early Irish Law 'Property Rights in Celtic Irish Law', *Journal of Libertarian Studies*, 1 (2), 81–95 in 1977. Much of what he had to say still stands. Since his article was published, a diplomatic edition of the surviving legal material has been published and an introductory but comprehensive guide to early Irish law was published by Fergus Kelly (1988), *A Guide to Early Irish Law* (Dublin: Dublin Institute for Advanced Studies). This was followed by Neil McLeod (1992), *Early Irish Contract Law* (Sydney: Centre for Celtic Studies), and Robin Chapman Stacey (1994), *The Road to Judgment: From Custom to Court in Medieval Ireland and Wales* (Philadelphia: University of Pennsylvania Press), so that we now have a much fuller and more detailed picture of how things were in medieval Ireland. None of this material contradicts any of Peden's substantive points.

49   The material immediately following is a précis of Kelly (1988).

50   The role of the king was quasi-sacerdotal, no doubt reflecting an earlier stage of social development, which persisted in other societies and recurred with surprising frequency until relatively recently, for example, the Chinese Emperor, the Egyptian Pharaoh, the Roman and Byzantine Emperors and the notion of the Divine Right of Kings.

51   See Richard R. Cherry (1883–84), 'The Eric Fines of Ancient Irish Law', *Journal of The Statistical and Social Inquiry Society of Ireland*, 8 (52), 544–51.

52   Kelly (1988), p. 21.

53   Peden (1977), p. 82.

54 Ibid., p. 83. He notes that while the Irish had kings, it is important to realise that they were not lawmakers. Kings were first among equals (freemen), not in a class apart. Moreover, they could be sued just as any other freeman could albeit with difficulty. Each freeman had what was known as his honour-price, his *dire* or *enclann*. This honour-price was essential to the working of the systems of sureties. In taking or in defending an action, a petitioner or a defendant took sureties to ensure the honouring of the judgement of the brehon court.

55 This section is based primarily on the work of Michael van Notten (2006), *The Law of the Somalis: A Stable Foundation for Economic Development in the Horn of Africa* (Trenton, NJ: Red Sea Press). See also Peter T. Leeson (2007a), 'Better off Stateless: Somalia before and after Government Collapse', available at www.peterleeson.com/better_off_stateless.pdf and (2007b), 'Anarchy Unbound, or: Why Self-Governance Works Better Than You Think', available at www.cato-unbound.org/2007/08/06/peter-t-leeson/anarchy-unbound-or-why-self-governance-works-better-than-you-think/.

56 Kritarchy is a term used to describe a politico-legal system that is based on the implementation of customary, non-statutory law in a society in which there is no fundamental distinction between rulers and ruled.

57 The *mag* of a man is 100 camels; of a woman, 50 if the homicide was intentional; 60–70 for a man and 30–35 for a woman if accidental or negligent.

58 For more material illustrating the existence of legal orders without the state, see Benson (1990a), and (1990b), Avner Greif (1989), 'Reputation and Coalitions in Medieval Trade: Evidence on the Maghribi Traders', *Journal of Economic History*, 44 (4), 857–82, Paul Milgrom, Douglass North and Barry Weingast (1990), 'The Role of Institutions in the Revival of Trade: the Medieval Law Merchant, Private Judges, and the Champagnes Fairs', in Edward Stringham (ed.), *Anarchy and the Law: The Political Economy of Choice* (New Brunswick: Transaction), 602–23, Thomas J. Thomson (2006), 'An Ancient Stateless Civilization: Bronze Age India and the State in History', *The Independent Review*, 10 (3), 365–84 and section IV of Stringham (2007), 'Historical Case Studies of Non-Government Law Enforcement', pp. 538–679.

59 See Thomas Whiston (2002), 'Medieval Iceland and the Absence of Government', available at www.mises.org/story/1121; Birgir T. Runolfsson Solvason (1990), 'Ordered Anarchy: Evolution of the Decentralized Legal Order in the Icelandic Commonwealth, 930–1264', available at http://

notendur.hi.is/bthru/iep.htm), and (1993), 'Institutional Evolution in the Icelandic Commonwealth' (*Constitutional Political Economy*), 4 (1), 97–125; Robert Murphy (2011a), 'But Wouldn't Warlords Take Over?', available at http://mises.org/daily/1855 and (2011b), 'Christopher Beam Takes On Libertarianism', available at http://mises.org/daily/4956; David Friedman (1979), 'Private Creation and Enforcement of Law – a Historical Case', *Journal of Legal Studies*, 8 (2), 399–415 and Roderick T. Long (2009), 'Privatization, Viking Style: Model or Misfortune?', available at www.lewrockwell.com/orig3/long1.html.

60 See Bruce Benson (1990b), *The Enterprise of Law: Justice without the State* (San Francisco: Pacific Research Institute for Public Policy), p. 21.

61 Benson 1989, p. 13.

62 Murray N. Rothbard (2006), *For a New Liberty*, 2nd edn (Auburn, AL: Ludwig von Mises Institute), pp. 282–3.

63 See Safner (No Date), available at http://ryansafner.com/publications/all-about-anarchism.

64 See the final chapter for more on the limits of constitutions. See Alfred G. Cuzan (1979), 'Do We Ever Really Get Out of Anarchy?', *The Journal of Libertarian Studies*, 3 (2), and Alfred G. Cuzan (2010), 'Revisiting "Do We Ever Really get out of Anarchy?" ', *The Journal of Libertarian Studies*, 22.

65 Ryan Safner (2011), 'All About Anarchism: I Can't Believe It's Not Chaos!', available at http://ryansafner.com/publications/all-about-anarchism/.

66 Tom W. Bell (1991–92), 'Polycentric Law', *Humane Studies Review*, 7 (1), pp. 1–2, pp. 4–10, (2002), 'The Jurisprudence of Polycentric Law', available at www.tomwbell.com/writings/JurisPoly.htm and (1998), 'Polycentric Law in a New Century', *Cato Policy Report*, XX (6), p. 1, pp. 10–11.

67 Parliament was originally not a law-making body but a tax-granting body opposed to the tax demands of the executive. After the 'Glorious Revolution' of 1689, as Parliament became subservient to an executive appointed from its own ranks, the opposition gradually disappeared so that tax levying became institutional and politically unopposed.

Chapter 6: Delegitimizing the state

1 Some parts of this chapter first appeared in Gerard Casey (2010b), 'Constitutions of No Authority: Spoonerian Reflections' and are reprinted with permission from the publisher of *The Independent Review: A Journal* *of Political Economy* (Winter 2010, XIV (3), pp. 325–40). Copyright 2010, The Independent Institute, 100 Swan Way, Oakland, CA 94621-1428 USA; info@independent.org; mailto:info@independent.org; info@independent.org, www.independent.org.

2 Whether this is so or not conceptually, psychologically it seems to be completely false. As Mencken remarks, 'The average man, whatever his errors otherwise, at least sees clearly that government is something lying outside him and outside the generality of his fellow men – that it is a separate, independent and often hostile power, only partly under his control, and capable of doing him great harm.' H. L. Mencken (ed.), (1982 [1916]), *A Mencken Chrestomathy* (New York: Vintage Books), p. 146.

3 Anthony de Jasay is well known for his critique of the possibility of a government that is really limited by a constitution. See Anthony de Jasay (2010c), 'The Concept of Rule-Bound Collective Choice and the Idea of Constitutional Safeguards', *Political Philosophy, Clearly: Essays on Freedom and Fairness, Property and Equalities* (Indianapolis: The Liberty Fund), pp. 231–54.

4 In this chapter, I concentrate on arguing democracy's lack of legitimacy. For a complementary treatment of some of the many other shortcomings of democracy, see Jan Narveson (2008), *You and the State: A Fairly Brief Introduction to Political Philosophy* (Lanham, MD: Rowman & Littlefield), pp. 115–34.

5 Part of this chapter began life in a somewhat different form as Gerard Casey (2009), '"Which is to be Master?": The Indefensibility of Political Representation', *Philosophical Inquiry*, 31 (3–4), 1–10.

6 These principles apply without modification only to fully autonomous adults. Children and non-autonomous adults (if there are any such), raise special problems. When I initially formulated these principles, principle 5, allowed only for compensation and not for specific performance. However, after a conversation with Walter Block on the topic of voluntary slavery, I am persuaded that there can be no legitimate objection to that principle's encompassing specific performance also.

7 Clarence S. Darrow (2011 [1903]), *Resist Not Evil* (Auburn, AL: Ludwig von Mises Institute), p. 4.

8 Francis Fukuyama (2011), *The Origins of Political Order* (London: Profile Books), p. 325. Before the twentieth century, not everyone was persuaded of the incontrovertible merits of democracy. See William Lecky (1981 [1896]), *Democracy and Liberty*, 2 vols (Indianapolis: Liberty Fund); Thomas Carlyle (2005 [1850]), *Latter-Day Pamphlets* (New York: Elibron

Classics); Henry Maine (1976 [1885]), *Popular Government* (Indianapolis: Liberty Fund); and, from the early part of the twentieth century, William Hurrell Mallock (1918), *The Limits of Pure Democracy* (London: Chapman and Hall, Ltd). For contemporary critiques of democracy, see Hans-Hermann Hoppe (2001), *Democracy: The God that Failed* (New Brunswick, NJ: Transaction), and Gordon Graham (2002), *The Case against the Democratic State* (Thorverton: Imprint Academic).

  9 Michael Bakunin (1871), 'On Science and Authority' in Robert Graham (ed.), (2005), *Anarchism: A Documentary History of Libertarian Ideas: Volume One: From Anarchy to Anarchism (300CE to 1939)* (London: Black Rose Books), pp. 89–92, p. 90.

10 Hobbes, Thomas (1996 [1651]), *Leviathan* (Cambridge: Cambridge University Press), p. 124.

11 Hanna Fenichel Pitkin (1967), *The Concept of Democracy* (Berkeley, CA: University of California Press).

12 Ibid., p. 2.

13 Ibid., p. 3.

14 I acknowledge here my obvious debt here to the thought of Lysander Spooner.

15 See Pitkin (1967), p. 215; pp. 219–20.

16 An instance of symbolic representation occurs when Elrond is choosing the Company of the Ring in Tolkien's *Lord of the Rings*. He says: 'For the rest, they shall represent the other Free Peoples of the World: Elves, Dwarves, and Men. Legolas shall be for the Elves; and Gimli, son of Gloin for the Dwarves. . . . For men you shall have Aragorn . . .' J. R. R. Tolkien (1969), *Lord of the Rings: The Fellowship of the Rings* (London: Harper Collins), p. 362.

17 An instance of religious representation can be seen when a Catholic priest is said to represent Christ in the sacrament of confession when he says, 'ego te absolvo . . .'.

18 Pitkin (1967), p. 221.

19 Ibid.

20 Ibid.

21 Ibid.

22 Ibid., pp. 221–2. She picks up this idea again when she says '. . . when we speak of political representation, we are almost always speaking of individuals acting in an institutionalized representative system, and it is against the background of that system as a whole that their action constitute representation, if they do'. (p. 225).

23 Lewis Carroll (1972 [1871]), *Through the Looking Glass* (London: Hart-Davis, MacGib, p. 81.

24 Lon L. Fuller (1964), *The Morality of Law* (New Haven, CT: Yale University Press), cited in Bruce L. Benson (1990a), 'Customary Law with Private Means of Resolving Disputes and Dispensing Justice: a Description of a Modern System of Law and Order without State Coercion', *The Journal of Libertarian Studies*, 9 (2), 25–42, 26.

25 Randy E. Barnett (1998), *The Structure of Liberty: Justice and the Rule of Law* (Oxford: Oxford University Press), p. 3

26 See N. Parpworth (2000), *Constitutional and Administrative Law* (London: Butterworths), p. 3.

27 Roderick T. Long 'Market Anarchism as Constitutionalism' in Roderick T. Long and T. Machan (eds), *Anarchism/Minarchism: Is Government Part of a Free Country?* (Aldershot, Hampshire: Ashgate Publishing), p. 140.

28 The other two possibilities are that it is a non-binding agreement or a non-binding non-agreement. The latter is as close to being nothing as makes no difference, and the former, though possible, could hardly function as the fundamental law of a state.

29 O. Handlin and M. Handlin (eds), (1966), *The Popular Sources of Political Authority: Documents on the Massachusetts Constitution of 1780* (Cambridge, MA: The Belknap Press.), p. 441.

30 Alfred Denning, Baron Denning, was one of the best known British judges of the twentieth century. He was notorious for his bold judgements, many of which were overturned by the House of Lords but some of which were later enacted into law by Parliament.

31 A deed is a legal instrument used to grant a right.

32 Promissory estoppel is a doctrine that purports to makes certain promises legally binding in the absence of consideration.

33 *Currie v Misa (1875)*, *LR 10 Ex 153*; (1875–76) LR 1 App Cas 554.

34 This is known as privity of contract.

35 George H. Smith (ed.), (1992), *The Lysander Spooner Reader* (San Francisco: Fox & Wilkes), p. 77; emphasis added.

36 See ibid., p. 77.

37 Ibid.

38 See Ibid., p. 65.

39 Ibid., p. 77.

40 Randy E. Barnett (2004), *Restoring the Lost Constitution* (Princeton, NJ: Princeton University Press), p. 24.

41 See A. John Simmons (1993), *On the Edge of Anarchy: Locke, Consent, and the Limits of Society* (Princeton, NJ: Princeton University Press), and A. John Simmons (2005), 'Consent Theory for Libertarians', *Social Philosophy and Policy*, 22 (1), 330–56, passim.

42 Simmons (1993), p. 255.

43 Again, see Simmons (1993), passim.

44 Ibid., p. 222.

45 Smith (1992), p. 67.

46 Ibid., p. 85. 'And yet we have what purports, or professes, or is claimed, to be a contract – the Constitution – made eighty years ago, by men who are now all dead, and who never had any power to bind us, but which (it is claimed), has nevertheless bound three generations of men, consisting of many millions, and which (it is claimed), will be binding upon all the millions that are to come; but which nobody ever signed, sealed, delivered, witnessed or acknowledged; and which few persons, compared with the whole number that are claimed to be bound by it, have ever read, or even seen, or ever will read, or see. And of those who ever have read it, or ever will read it, scarcely any two, perhaps no two, have ever agreed, or ever will agree, as to what it means.' Smith (1992), p. 91.

47 Simmons (1993), p. 247.

48 F. M. Turner (ed.), (2002 [1790]), *Burke's Reflections on the Revolution in France* (New Haven, CT: Yale University Press), pp. 82–3.

49 Ibid.

50 Ibid.

51 Ibid.

52 Edmund Burke (1854–56), *The Works of the Right Honourable Edmund Burke.* 6 vols. Speech on Conciliation with the Colonies (1745)–vol. I (London: Henry G. Bohn), pp. 464–71.

53 Turner (2002), pp. xiv–xv.

54 Ibid., p. 219.

55 Ibid., p. 24.

56 Ibid., p. xxv.

57 Henry Sumner Maine (1906), *Ancient Law, its Connection with the Early History of Society and its Relation to Modern Ideas, with an introduction and notes by Sir Frederick Pollock.* 4th American from 10th London edn (New York: Henry Holt and Co.), chapter 5, paragraph 128.

Chapter 7: Conclusion

1 Aristotle (1998), *Nicomachean Ethics.* trans. David Ross (Oxford: Oxford University Press) (1094b19–23).

BIBLIOGRAPHY

Ackerman, B. A. (1980) *Social Justice in the Liberal State*. New Haven, CT: Yale University Press.

Adams, C. (1998) *Those Dirty Rotten Taxes*. New York: Simon & Schuster.

Ames, E. and R. T. Rapp (1977) 'The Birth and Death of Taxes: A Hypothesis', *Journal of Economic History,* 37 (1), 161–78.

Anderson, T. L. and P. J. Hill (1979) 'An American Experiment in Anarcho-Capitalism: The *not* So Wild, Wild West', *The Journal of Libertarian Studies,* 3 (1), 9–29.

—. (2004) *The Not So Wild Wild West: Property Rights on the Frontier*. Stanford, CA: Stanford University Press.

Anon. (No Date) 'Replies to some Errors and Distortions in Bryan Caplan's "Anarchist Theory FAQ" version 5.2', available at www.spunk.org/texts/intro/faq/sp001547/append1.html.

—. (ed.) (2010) *Anarchist Academics: Noam Chomsky, David D. Friedman, Murray Rothbard, Howard Zinn, Peter Neville, Jan Narveson, Murray Bookchin*. Memphis, TN: Books LLC.

—. (2011a) 'Who Needs Government? Pirates, Collapsed States, and the Possibility of Anarchy' available at www.cato-unbound.org/archives/august-2007/.

—. (2011b) 'An Anarchist FAQ – F.1 Are "Anarcho"–Capitalists really Anarchists?' available at www.infoshop.org/page/AnarchistFAQSectionF1.

—. (2011c) 'Somalia: 20 Years of Anarchy', available at www.bbc.co.uk/news/world-africa-12285365.

Aquinas, St T. (1946) *Summa Theologica*. New York: Benziger Brothers.

Aristotle. (1998) *Nicomachean Ethics*. Trans. David Ross. Oxford: Oxford University Press, (1094b19–23).

Baker, J. H. (2007) *An Introduction to English Legal History*, 4th edn. Oxford: Oxford University Press.

Baker, L. R. (1987) *Saving Belief: A Critique of Physicalism*. Princeton, NJ: Princeton University Press.

Bakunin, M. (1871) 'On Science and Authority' in Robert Graham (ed.) (2005) *Anarchism: A Documentary History of Libertarian Ideas: Volume One: From Anarchy to Anarchism (300CE to 1939)*. London: Black Rose Books, 89–92.

Barden, G. and T. Murphy (2010) *Law and Justice in Community*. Oxford: Oxford University Press.

Barnett, H. (1998) *Constitutional and Administrative Law*, 2nd edn. London: Cavendish Publishing.

Barnett, R. E. (1998) *The Structure of Liberty: Justice and the Rule of Law*. Oxford: Oxford University Press.

—. (2004) *Restoring the Lost Constitution*. Princeton, NJ: Princeton University Press.

Bastiat, F. (1995 [1848]) *Selected Essays on Political Economy*. Trans. Seymour Cain. Irvington-on-Hudson, NY: The Foundation for Economic Education.

Beam, C. (2011) 'The Trouble with Liberty', available at http://nymag.com/news/politics/70282/.

Becker, L. C. (1977) *Property Rights: Philosophic Foundations*. London: Routledge & Kegan Paul.

Bell, T. W. (1991–2) 'Polycentric Law', *Humane Studies Review,* 7 (1), 1–2, 4–10, available at http://osf1.gmu.edu/~ihs/w91issues.html.

—. (1998) 'Polycentric Law in a New Century', *Cato Policy Report,* XX (6), 1, 10–11.

—. (2009) 'The Jurisprudence of Polycentric Law', available at www.tomwbell.com/writings/JurisPoly.htm.

Benson, B. L. (1986) 'Guns for Protection, and Other Private Sector Responses to the Government's Failure to Control Crime', *The Journal of Libertarian Studies,* 8 (1), 75–109.

—. (1989) 'Enforcement of Private Property Rights in Primitive Societies', *The Journal of Libertarian Studies,* 9, 1–26.

—. (1990a) 'Customary Law with Private Means of Resolving Disputes and Dispensing Justice: A Description of a Modern System of Law and Order without State Coercion', *The Journal of Libertarian Studies,* 9 (2), 25–42.

—. (1990b) *The Enterprise of Law: Justice without the State*. San Francisco: Pacific Research Institute for Public Policy.

—. (1991a) 'An Evolutionary Contractarian View of Primitive law: The Institutions and Incentives Arising under Customary Indian Law', *The Review of Austrian Economics,* 5 (1), 41–65.

—. (1991b) 'Reciprocal Exchange as the Basis for Recognition of Law: Examples from American History', *The Journal of Libertarian Studies,* 10 (1), 53–82.

—. (1998) *To Serve and Protect: Privatization and Community in Criminal Justice*. New York: New York University Press.

Beran, H. (1977) 'In Defense of the Consent Theory of Political Obligation and Authority', *Ethics,* 87 (3), 260–71.

—. (1987) *The Consent Theory of Political Obligation*. London: Croom Helm.

Bergland, D. (1990) *Libertarianism in One Lesson*, 5th edn. Costa Mesa, CA: Orpheus Publications.

Berman, H. J. (1983) *Law and Revolution*. Cambridge, MA: Harvard University Press.

—. (2003) *Law and Revolution II: The Impact of the Protestant Reformations on the Western Legal Tradition*. Cambridge, MA: Belnap Press.

Berns, W. (1984) 'The Need for Public Authority', in G. W. Carey (ed.), *Freedom and Virtue: The Conservative/Libertarian debate*. Lanham, MD: University Press of America, 25–33.

Bill, H. (2011) 'Anarcho-Capitalist FAQ', available at www.ozarkia.net/bill/anarchism/faq.html.

Birch, P. (2011a) 'A Fatal Instability in Anarcho-Capitalism', available at www.paulbirch.net/AnarchoCapitalism1.html.

—. (2011b) 'Anarcho-Capitalism Dissolves into City States', available at www.paulbirch.net/AnarchoCapitalism2.html.

—. (2011c) 'Is Anarcho-Capitalism possible?', available at www.paulbirch.net/AnarchoCapitalism3.html.

Block, W. E. (2003) 'Towards a Libertarian Theory of Inalienability: A Critique of Rothbard, Barnett, Smith, Kinsella, Gordon, and Epstein', *Journal of Libertarian Studies,* 17 (2), 39–85.

—. (2006) 'Kevin Carson as Dr. Jekyll and Mr. Hyde', *The Journal of Libertarian Studies,* 20 (1), 35–46.

—. (2008 [1976]) *Defending the Undefendable.* Auburn, AL: Ludwig von Mises Institute.

—. (2010) 'Libertarianism is Unique and Belongs Neither to the Right nor the Left: A Critique of the Views of Long, Holcombe, and Baden on the Left, Hoppe, Feser and Paul on the Right', *The Journal of Libertarian Studies,* 22, 127–70.

Boaz, D. (1997) *The Libertarian Reader*. New York: The Free Press.

Brockman, J. (ed.) (2006) *What We Believe But Cannot Prove*. London: Pocket Books.

Brown, A. (2009) *Personal Responsibility: Why It Matters*. London: Continuum.

Browne, H. (1995) *Why Government Doesn't Work*. New York: St Martin's Press.

Buchanan, M. (2011) 'Peers Concern at "Tsunami" of New Legislation', *BBC News UK Politics*, available at www.bbc.co.uk/news/uk-politics-14794400.

Buckle, S. (1991) *Natural Law and the Theory of Property*. Oxford: Clarendon Press.

Burke, E. (1854–6) *The Works of the Right Honourable Edmund Burke. 6 vols. Speech on Conciliation with the Colonies (1745)–vol. I, 464–471*. London: Henry G. Bohn.

Caplan, B. (No Date) 'Appendix: Defining Anarchism', available at http://econfaculty.gmu.edu/bcaplan/def.htm.

—. (2011) 'Anarchist Theory FAQ', available at http://econfaculty.gmu.edu/bcaplan/anarfaq.htm.

Carey, G. W. (ed.) (1984) *Freedom and Virtue: The Conservative/Libertarian Debate*. Lanham, MD: Intercollegiate Studies Institute.

Carkuff, D. (2010) 'Libertarianism is Kidstuff', available at www.ncc-1776.org/tle2010/tle556–20100207-05.html.

Carlyle, T. (2005 [1850]) *Latter-Day Pamphlets*. New York: Elibron Classics.

Carroll, L. (1972 [1871]) *Through the Looking Glass*. London: Hart-Davis, MacGibbon.

Carter, J. C. (1907) *Law: Its Origin, Growth and Function*. New York: G. P. Putnam's Sons.

Casey, G. (1989) 'Angelic Interiority', *Irish Philosophical Journal,* 6 (1), 82–118.

—. (2003) 'Ethics and Human Nature', *American Catholic Philosophical Quarterly,* 77 (4), 519–31.

—. (2007) 'Meddling in Other Men's Affairs', *Economic Affairs*, 27 (4), 46–51.

—. (2009) '"Which is to be Master?": The Indefensibility of Political Representation', *Philosophical Inquiry,* 31 (3–4), 1–10.

—. (2010a) 'Reflections on Legal Polycentrism', *Journal of Libertarian Studies,* 22, 22–34.

—. (2010b) 'Constitutions of No Authority: Spoonerian Reflections', *Independent Review,* 14 (3), 325–40.

—. (2010c) *Murray Rothbard*. New York: Continuum.

—. (2011) 'Libertarianism and Conservatism: Friends or Foes?', in D. Ozsel (ed.), *Reflections on Conservatism*. Cambridge: Cambridge Scholars Publishing, 22–45.

—. (2012) 'The Inescapability of Ethics', forthcoming in F. O'Rourke *What Happened in and to Moral Philosophy in the Twentieth Century?: Philosophical Essays in Honour of Alisdair Macintyre*. Notre Dame, Indiana: University of Notre Dame Press.

Cherry, R. R. (1883–4) 'The Eric Fines of Ancient Irish Law', *Journal of The Statistical and Social Inquiry Society of Ireland,* 8 (52), 544–51.

Cicero, M. T. (1998) *The Republic and The Laws.* Trans. Niall Rudd. Oxford: Oxford University Press.

Cohen, G. A. (1995) *Self-Ownership, Freedom and Equality.* Cambridge: Cambridge University Press.

Collingwood, R. G. (1940) *Metaphysics.* Oxford: Clarendon Press.

Cuzan, A. G. (1979) 'Do We Ever Really Get Out of Anarchy?', *The Journal of Libertarian Studies,* 3 (2), 151–58.

—. (2010) 'Revisiting "Do We Ever Really get out of Anarchy?"', *The Journal of Libertarian Studies,* 22 (3–21).

Darrow, C. S. (2011 [1903]) *Resist Not Evil.* Auburn, AL: Ludwig von Mises Institute.

Darwin, Charles. (1881 [1897]) 'Letter to William Graham, 3 July 1881', in Francis Darwin (ed.), *The Life and Letters of Charles Darwin,* 3 vols. London: John Murray.

Davies, S. (2002) 'The Private Provision of Police during the Eighteenth and Nineteenth Centuries', in David T. Beito, Peter Gordon, and Alexander T. Tabarrok (eds), *The Voluntary City: Choice, Community and Civil Society.* Oakland, CA: The Independent Institute, 151–81.

de Jasay, A. (1997) *Against Politics: On Government, Anarchy and Order.* London: Routledge.

—. (2010a) *Political Philosophy, Clearly: Essays on Freedom and Fairness, Property and Equalities.* Hartmut Kliemt (ed.). Indianapolis: The Liberty Fund.

—. (2010b) 'Freedom, from a Mainly Logical Perspective', in Hartmut Kliemt (ed.), *Political Philosophy, Clearly: Essays on Freedom and Fairness, Property and Equalilties.* Indianapolis: The Liberty Fund, 206–27.

—. (2010c) 'The Concept of Rule-Bound Collective Choice and the Idea of Constitutional Safeguards', in Hartmut Kliemt (ed.), *Political Philosophy, Clearly: Essays on Freedom and Fairness, Property and Equalilties.* Indianapolis: The Liberty Fund, 231–54.

de Jouvenal, B. (1955) *Sovereignty: An Inquiry into the Political Good.* Chicago: University of Chicago Press.

de Molinari, G. (1904) *The Society of Tomorrow: A Forecast of Its Political and Economic Organization.* London: T. Fisher Unwin.

—. (2007 [1849]) 'The Production of Security', in Edward Stringham (ed.), *Anarchy and the Law: The Political Economy of Choice.* London: Transaction Publishers.

de Wolf, A. (2011) 'Review of de Jasay's Political Philosophy, Clearly', *Economic Affairs,* 31 (2), 107–08.

Deutsch, B. (2011) 'The 24 Types of Libertarian', available at www.leftycartoons.com/the-24-types-of-libertarian/.

Dillon, M. and N. Chadwick (1967) *Celtic Realms.* London: Weidenfeld & Nicholson.

Down, K. (1997) 'Anarchy, Warfare, and Social Order', *The Journal of Political Economy* 105 (3), 648–51.

Duncan, C. and T. Machan (2005) *Libertarianism: For and Against.* Lanham, MD: Rowman & Littlefield.

Ellickson, R. C. (1991) *Order without Law: How Neighbors Settle Disputes.* Cambridge, MA: Harvard University Press.

Emsley, C. (2010) *The Great British Bobby: A History of British Policing from the 18th Century to the Present.* London: Quercus.

Ertman, T. (1997) *Birth of the Leviathan: Building States and Regimes in Medieval and Early Modern Europe.* Cambridge: Cambridge University Press.

Evans, P., D. Rueschemeyer and T. Skocpol (eds) (1985) *Bringing the State Back In.* Cambridge: Cambridge University Press.

Feser, E. (2005) 'There's No Such Thing as an Unjust Initial Acquisition', *Social Philosophy and Policy,* 22 (1), 56–80.

—. (2010) 'Classical Natural Law Theory, Property Rights, and Taxation', *Social Philosophy and Policy,* 27 (1), 21–52.

Fielding, K. T. (1978) 'Stateless Society: Frech on Rothbard', *Journal of Libertarian Studies,* 2 (2), 179–81.

Fitzgerald, R. (2003) *Mugged by the State: Outrageous Government Assaults on Ordinary People and their Property.* Washington, DC: Regnery Publishing.

Fried, C. (2007) *Modern Liberty and the Limits of Government.* New York and London: W. W. Norton & Company.

Friedman, D. (1979) 'Private Creation and Enforcement of Law–a Historical Case', *Journal of Legal Studies,* 8 (2), 399–415.

—. (1989) *The Machinery of Freedom: Guide to a Radical Capitalism,* 2nd edn. La Salle, IL: Open Court.

Fukuyama, F. (2010) 'Transitions to the Rule of Law', *Journal of Democracy,* 21 (1), 33–44.

—. (2011) *The Origins of Political Order.* London: Profile Books.

Fuller, L. L. (1964) *The Morality of Law.* New Haven, CT: Yale University Press.

—. (1978) 'The Form and Limits of Adjudication', *Harvard Law Review,* 92 (2), 353–409.

Graham, G. (2002) *The Case against the Democratic State*. Thorverton: Imprint Academic.

Graham, R. (ed.) (2005) *Anarchism: A Documentary History of Libertarian Ideas: Volume One: From Anarchy to Anarchism (300CE to 1939)*. London: Black Rose Books.

—. (ed.) (2007) *Anarchism: A Documentary History of Libertarian Ideas: Volume Two: The Anarchist Current (1939–2006)*. London: Black Rose Books.

Greif, A. (1989) 'Reputation and Coalitions in Medieval Trade: Evidence on the Maghribi Traders', *Journal of Economic History,* 44 (4), 857–82.

Grotius, H. (1925 [1646]) *De Jure Belli ac Pacis*. Trans. Francis W. Kelsey. Oxford: Clarendon Press.

Grunebaum, J. O. (1986) *Private Ownership*. London: Routledge.

Halliday, R. (2011) 'Historical Examples of Anarchy without Chaos', available at http://royhalliday.home.mindspring.com/history.htm.

Harsanyi, D. (2007) *Nanny State: How Food Fascists, Teetotaling Do-Gooders, Priggish Moralists, and Other Boneheaded Bureaucrats are turning America into a Nation of Children*. New York: Broadway Books.

Hart, H. L. A. (1994 [1961]) *The Concept of Law*, 2nd edn. Oxford: The Clarendon Press.

Hasnas, J. (2008) 'The Obviousness of Anarchy', in Roderick T. Long and Tibor R. Machan, (eds) (2008) *Anarchism/Miniarchism: Is Government Part of a Free Country?* Aldershot, Hampshire: Ashgate Publishing.

Hayek, F. A. (1946) 'Individualism: True and False (Given as the 12th Finlay Lecture in University College Dublin in 1945)', *Individualism and Economic Order*. Chicago: University of Chicago Press.

—. (1948) *Individualism and Economic Order*. Chicago: University of Chicago Press.

—. (1976) *Law, Legislation, and Liberty: The Mirage of Social Justice*. Chicago: University of Chicago Press.

—. (1982) *Law, Legislation and Liberty: A New Statement of the Liberal Principles of Justice and Political Economy*. London: Routledge.

Herzog, D. (1989) *Happy Slaves: A Critique of Consent Theory*. Chicago: University of Chicago Press.

Higgs, R. (2004) *Against Leviathan: Government Power and a Free Society.* Oakland, CA: Independent Institute.

Hobbes, T. (1996 [1651]) *Leviathan*. Cambridge: Cambridge University Press.

Hoebel, E. A. (1954) *The Law of Primitive Man*. Cambridge, MA: Harvard University Press.

Hoffman, John. (1995) *Beyond the State: An Introductory Critique*. Cambridge: Polity Press.

Hogan, G. and G. Whyte (1994) *The Irish Constitution*, 3rd edn. Dublin: Butterworths.

—. (2003) *J M Kelly: The Irish Constitution*, 4th edn. Dublin: LexisNexis Butterworths.

Hohfeld, W. N. (1923) *Fundamental Legal Conceptions as Applied in Judicial Reasoning and Other Essays*. Walter Wheeler Cook (ed.). New Haven, CT: Yale University Press.

Honderich, T. (1990) *Conservatism*. London: Penguin.

Hoppe, H.-H. (2001) *Democracy: The God that Failed*. New Brunswick, NJ: Transaction Publishers.

—. (2003) *The Myth of National Defense*. Auburn, AL: Mises Institute.

Hornberger, J. G. (2011) 'Conservatism vs. Libertarianism', available at www. fff.org/comment/com0604c.asp.

Huebert, J. H. (2010) *Libertarianism Today*. Oxford: Praeger.

Hufton, O. (1994) *Europe: Privilege and Protest 1730–1789*. London: Fontana Press.

Hughes, K. (1966) *The Church in Early Irish Society*. London: Menthuen.

Hume, D. (1826 [1748]) 'Of the Original Contract', in T. H. Green and T. H. Grose (eds), *Essays Moral, Political, and Literary*. London: Longmans and Green.

Infoshop.org (1995) 'An Anarchist FAQ', available at www.infoshop.org/page/AnAnarchistFAQ.

Kant, I. (1963 [1786]) 'The Conjectural Beginnings of Human History', in Lewis White Beck (ed.), *Kant: On History*. New York: Bobbs-Merrill, 53–68.

—. (1996 [1797]) *The Metaphysics of Morals*. Trans. Mary Gregor. Cambridge: Cambridge University Press.

Kekes, J. (2010) 'The Right to Private Property: A Justification', *Social Philosophy and Policy*, 27 (1), 1–20.

Kelly, F. (1988) *A Guide to Early Irish Law*. Dublin: Dublin Institute for Advanced Studies.

Kennedy, J. T. (2011) 'The Fundamental Fallacy of Government', available at www.anti-state.com/kennedy/kennedy1.html.

Kinsella, S. (2011) 'What Libertarianism Is', available at http://mises.org/daily/3660.

Kirk, R. (1984) 'Libertarians: The Chirping Sectaries', in Carey, George W. (ed.) (1984) *Freedom and Virtue: The Conservative/Libertarian debate*. Lanham, MD: Intercollegiate Studies Institute.

Lane, T. (1996) 'On Anarchism: Noam Chomsky Interviewed by Tom Lane', available at www.chomsky.info/interviews/19961223.htm.

Lecky, W. (1981 [1896]) *Democracy and Liberty*, 2 vols. Indianapolis: Liberty Fund.

Leeson, P. T. (2007a) 'Better off Stateless: Somalia Before and After Government Collapse', available at www.peterleeson.com/better_off_stateless.pdf.

—. (2007b) 'Anarchy Unbound, or: Why Self-Governance Works Better Than You Think', available at www.cato-unbound.org/2007/08/06/peter-t-leeson/anarchy-unbound-or-why-self-governance-works-better-than-you-think/.

Lester, J. C. (2000) *Escape from Leviathan: Liberty, Welfare and Anarchy Reconsidered*. London: Macmillan.

Llewellyn, K. N. and E. A. Hoebel (1941) *The Cheyenne Way*. Norman, OK: University of Oklahoma Press.

Long, R. T. (2008) 'Market Anarchism as Constitutionalism', in Roderick T. Long and T. Machan (eds), *Anarchism/Minarchism: Is Government Part of a Free Country?* Aldershot, Hampshire: Ashgate Publishing.

—. (2009) 'Privatization, Viking Style: Model or Misfortune?', available at www.lewrockwell.com/orig3/long1.html.

—. (2011a) 'How to Reach the Left', available at http://mises.org/daily/5226/How-to-Reach-the-Left.

—. (2011b) 'Libertarian Anarchism: Responses to Ten Objections', available at www.lewrockwell.com/long/long11.html.

Long, R. T. and T. R. Machan (eds) (2008) *Anarchism/Miniarchism: Is Government Part of a Free Country?* Aldershot, Hampshire: Ashgate Publishing.

Machan, T. (1984) 'Libertarianism: The Principle of Liberty', in G. W. Carey (ed.), *Freedom and Virtue: The Conservative/Libertarian debate*. Lanham, MD: University Press of America, 35–58.

Machan, T. R. (2002) 'Anarchism and Minarchism: a Rapprochement', *Journal des économistes et des études humaines,* 12 (4), 569–88.

Machan, T. and D. B. Rasmussen (eds) (1995) *Liberty for the 21st Century: Contemporary Libertarian Thought*. Lanham, MD: Rowman & Littlefield Inc.

Mack, E. (1995) 'The Self-Ownership Proviso: A New and Improved Lockean Proviso', *Social Philosophy and Policy,* 12 (1), 186–218.

—. (2010) 'The Natural Right to Property', *Social Philosophy and Policy,* 27 (1), 53–78.

Maine, H. S. (1871) *Village-Communities in the East and West: Six Lectures delivered at Oxford*. London: John Murray.

—. (1890 [1883]) *On Early Law and Custom*. London: John Murray.

—. (1906) *Ancient Law, Its Connection with the Early History of Society and Its Relation to Modern Ideas, with an Introduction and Notes by Sir Frederick Pollock.* 4th American from 10th London edn. New York: Henry Holt and Co.

—. (1976 [1885]) *Popular Government*. Indianapolis: Liberty Fund.

Mallock, W. H. (1918) *The Limits of Pure Democracy*. London: Chapman and Hall, Ltd.

McElroy, W. (2011) 'American Anarchism', available at www.independent.org/issues/article.asp?id=10.

McGinn, C. (2000) *The Mysterious Flame: Conscious Minds in a Material World*. New York: Basic Books.

McKendrick, E. (ed.) (2009) *Goode on Commercial Law*. London: LexisNexis.

McLeod, N. (1992) *Early Irish Contract Law*. Sydney: Centre for Celtic Studies.

Mencken, H. L. (ed.) (1982 [1916]) *A Mencken Chrestomathy*. New York: Vintage Books.

Micklethwait, B. (1981) 'Anarchy versus Anarcho-Capitalism', *Political Notes,* (4), available at www.libertarian.co.uk/lapubs/polin/polin004.pdf.

Milgrom, P., D. North and B. Weingast (1990) 'The Role of Institutions in the Revival of Trade: The Medieval Law Merchant, Private Judges, and the Champagnes Fairs', in Edward Stringham (ed.), *Anarchy and the Law: The Political Economy of Choice*. New Brunswick: Transaction Publishers, 602–23.

Mill, J. S. (1974) *On Liberty*. London: Penguin.

Miron, J. A. (2010) *Libertarianism, from A to Z*. New York: Basic Books.

Moellendorf, D. (2011) 'World Ownership, Self-Ownership, and Equality in Georgist Philosophy', available at http://schalkenbach.org/scholars-forum/Tideman-Reply-to-Moellendorf.pdf.

Murdoch, I. (1994) *Metaphysics as a Guide to Morals*. London: Penguin.

Murphy, R. P. (2002) *Chaos Theory: Two Essays on Market Anarchy*. New York: RJ Communications LLC.

—. (2009) 'The Possibility of Private Law', available at www.mises.org/story/1874.

—. (2011a) 'But Wouldn't Warlords Take Over?', available at http://mises.org/daily/1855.

—. (2011b) 'Christopher Beam Takes On Libertarianism', available at http://mises.org/daily/4956.

—. (2011c) 'Anarchy in Somalia', available at http://mises.org/daily/5418/Anarchy-in-Somalia.

Murray, C. (1992) *What It Means to be a Libertarian*. Peterborough, ON: Broadway.

Narveson, J. (2001) *The Libertarian Idea*. Peterborough, ON: Broadway.

—. (2008) *You and the State: A Fairly Brief Introduction to Political Philosophy*. Lanham, MD: Rowman & Littlefield Publishers.

—. (2010) 'Property and Rights', *Social Philosophy and Policy,* 27 (1), 101–34.

Nenova, T. and T. Harford 'Anarchy and Invention (Note 280 in Public Policy for the Private Sector)', *Public Policy for the Private Sector,* available at http://rru.worldbank.org/PublicPolicyJournal.

Nisbet, R. (1984) 'Conservatives and Libertarians: Uneasy Cousins', in G. W. Carey (ed.), *Freedom and Virtue: The Conservative/Libertarian Debate.* Lanham, MD: University Press of America, 13–24.

Nock, A. J. (1928) *On Doing the Right Thing.* New York: Harper & Brothers Publishers.

Novak, D. (1958) 'The Place of Anarchism in the History of Political Thought', *The Review of Politics,* 20 (3), 307–29.

Nozick, R. (1974) *Anarchy, State and Utopia.* New York: Basic Books.

Olson, M. (1993) 'Dictatorship, Democracy, and Development', *American Political Science Review,* 87 (9), 567–76.

Opitz, E. A. (ed.) (1995) *Leviathan at War.* Irvington-on-Hudson: The Foundation for Economic Freedom.

Oppenheimer, F. (1975 [1919]) *The State.* Trans. John Gitterman. New York: Free Life Editions.

Osterfeld, D. (2007) 'Freedom, Society, and the State: An Investigation Into the Possibility of Society without Government (excerpt)', in Edward Stringham (ed.) (2007) *Anarchy and the Law: The Political Economy of Choice.* New Brunswick: Transaction Publishers.

Otsuka, M. (2003) *Libertarianism without Inequality.* Oxford: Clarendon Press.

Paine, T. (1995 [1776]) *Rights of Man & Common Sense.* Mark Philip (ed.). Oxford: Oxford University Press.

Palmer, T. (1998) 'G. A. Cohen on Self-Ownership, Property, and Equality', *Critical Review,* 12 (3), 225–51.

Parpworth, N. (2000) *Constitutional and Administrative Law.* London: Butterworths.

Peden, J. R. (1977) 'Property Rights in Celtic Irish Law ', *Journal of Libertarian Studies,* 1 (2), 81–95.

Peron, J. (2001) 'Are There Two Libertarianisms?', *Freeman,* 51 (6), 39–42.

Pitkin, H. F. (1967) *The Concept of Democracy.* Berkeley, CA: University of California Press.

Poggi, G. (1990) *The State: Its Nature, Development and Prospects.* Cambridge: Polity Press.

Powell, B., R. Ford and A. Nowrasteh (2006) 'Somalia after State Collapse: Chaos or Improvement?', The Independent Institute Working Paper 64, available at www.independent.org/pdf/working_papers/64_somalia.pdf.

Pritchard, A. M. (1961) *Leage's Roman Private Law*, 3rd edn. London: Macmillan & Co. Ltd.

Puzo, M. (1969) *The Godfather.* London: William Heinemann Ltd.

Raico, R. (2006) 'Classical Liberal Roots of the Marxist Doctrine of Classes', available at http://mises.org/daily/2217.

Richman, S. (2011) 'Libertarian Left', *The American Conservative*, available at www.amconmag.com/blog/libertarian-left/.

Riggenbach, J. (2011a) 'The New Libertarian Generation', available at http://mises.org/daily/4463.

—. (2011b) 'The Ignorance of New York Magazine', available at http://mises.org/daily/4990/The-Ignorance-of-iNew-Yorki-Magazine.

Rogers, T. (2010) 'Self-Ownership, World-Ownership, and Initial Acquisition', *Libertarian Papers,* 2 (36), 1–20.

Rose, C. M. (1985) 'Possession as the Origin of Property', *The University of Chicago Law Review,* 52 (1), 73–88.

Rothbard, M. N. (1973) 'A Future of Peace and Capitalism', in James H. Weaver (ed.), *Modern Political Economy.* Boston: Allyn and Bacon.

—. (1975) 'Society Without a State', *The Libertarian Forum,* 7 (1), 3–7.

—. (1984) 'Frank S. Meyer: The Fusionist as Libertarian Manqué', in G. W. Carey (ed.), *Freedom and Virtue: The Conservative/Libertarian Debate.* Lanham, MD: The University Press of America, 91–111.

—. (1994) 'Nations by Consent: Decomposing the Nation State', *The Journal of Libertarian Studies,* 11 (1), 1–10.

—. (2002 [1982]) *The Ethics of Liberty.* New York: New York University Press.

—. (2006) *For a New Liberty,* 2nd edn. Auburn, AL: Ludwig von Mises Institute.

Runolfsson Solvason, B. T. (1990) 'Ordered Anarchy: Evolution of the Decentralized Legal Order in the Icelandic Commonwealth, 930–1264', available at http://notendur.hi.is/bthru/iep.htm.

—. (1993) 'Institutional Evolution in the Icelandic commonwealth', *Constitutional Political Economy,* 4 (1), 97–125.

Safner, R. (2011) 'All About Anarchism: I Can't Believe It's Not Chaos!', available at http://ryansafner.com/publications/all-about-anarchism.

Sanders, J. and J. Narveson (1996) *For and Against the State.* Lanham, MD: Rowman & Littlefield.

Sartwell, C. (2008) *Against the State.* Albany, NY: State University of New York Press.

Schmidtz, D. (2006) *Elements of Justice.* Cambridge: Cambridge University Press.

Schmidtz, D. and J. Brennan (2010) *A Brief History of Liberty.* Oxford: Wiley-Blackwell.

Scott, J. C. (1985) *Weapons of the Weak: Everyday Forms of Peasant Resistance.* New Haven, CT: Yale University Press.

—. (1998) *Seeing Like a State: How Certain Schemes to Improve the Human Condition Have Failed.* New Haven, CT: Yale University Press.

—. (2009) *The Art of Not Being Governed.* New Haven, CT: Yale University Press.

Scruton, R. (1984) *The Meaning of Conservatism*, 2nd edn. London: Macmillan.

Simmons, A. J. (1993) *On the Edge of Anarchy: Locke, Consent, and the Limits of Society.* Princeton, NJ: Princeton University Press.

—. (2005) 'Consent Theory for Libertarians', *Social Philosophy and Policy,* 22 (1), 330–56.

Skoble, A. J. (1995) 'The Anarchism Controversy', in T. Machan and D. B. Rasmussen (eds), *Liberty for the 21st Century: Contemporary Libertarian Thought.* Lanham, MD: Rowman & Littlefield Inc., 77–96.

—. (2008a) 'Radical Freedom and Social Living', in Roderick T. Long and T. Machan (eds), *Anarchism/Minarchism: Is a Government part of a Free Country?*, 87–102.

—. (2008b) *Deleting the State: An Argument about Government.* Chicago: Open Court.

Smith, A. (1976 [1776]) *An Inquiry into the Nature and Causes of the Wealth of Nations*, R. H. Campbell, A. S. Skinner, and W. B. Todd (eds), 2 vols. Oxford: Clarendon Press.

—. (1978 [1762/1766]) *Lectures on Jurisprudence*, R. L. Meek, D. D. Raphael, and P. G. Stein (eds). Oxford: Oxford University Press.

Smith, G. H. (ed.) (1992) *The Lysander Spooner Reader.* San Francisco: Fox & Wilkes.

Sneed, J. D. (1977) 'Order without Law: Where will Anarchists Keep the Madmen?', *Journal of Libertarian Studies,* 1 (2), 117–24.

Spooner, L. (1870 [1992]) 'No Treason (No. VI): "The Constitution of No Authority"', in G. H. Smith (ed.), *The Lysander Spooner Reader.* San Francisco: Fox & Wilkes, 77–122.

Stacey, R. C. (1994) *The Road to Judgment: From Custom to Court in Medieval Ireland and Wales.* Philadelphia: University of Pennsylvania Press.

Stringham, E. (1998–9) 'Market Chosen Law', *Journal of Libertarian Studies,* 14 (1), 53–77.

—. (ed.) (2007) *Anarchy and the Law: The Political Economy of Choice.* New Brunswick: Transaction Publishers.

Tannehill, L. and M. Tannehill (1970) *The Market for Liberty.* San Francisco: Fox & Wilkes.

Taylor, Robert S. (2004) 'A Kantian Defense of Self-Ownership', *The Journal of Political Philosophy,* 12 (1), 65–78.

Thomson, T. J. (2006) 'An Ancient Stateless Civilization: Bronze Age India and the State in History', *The Independent Review,* 10 (3), 365–84.

Tilly, C. (1985) 'War Making and State Making as Organized Crime', in Peter Evans, Dietrich Rueschemeyer, and Theda Skocpol (eds), *Bringing the State Back In*. Cambridge: Cambridge University Press, 169–87.

—. (1992 [1990]) *Coercion, Capital and European States, AD 990–1992*. Revised edn. Oxford: Blackwell.

Tolkien, J. R. R. (1969) *Lord of the Rings: The Fellowship of the Rings*. London: Harper Collins.

Turner, F. M. (ed.) (2002 [1790]) *Burke's Reflections on the Revolution in France*. New Haven, CT: Yale University Press.

Vallentyne, P. (2010) 'Libertarianism', in Edward N. Zalta (ed.), *The Stanford Encyclopedia of Philosophy*.

van Dun, F. (2001) 'Natural Law, Liberalism, and Christianity', *The Journal of Libertarian Studies,* 15 (3), 1–36.

—. (2006) 'What is Kritarchy?', in Michael van Notten *The Law of the Somalis: A Stable Foundation for Economic Development in the Horn of Africa*. Trenton, NJ: Red Sea Press, 187–96.

van Notten, M. (2006) *The Law of the Somalis: A Stable Foundation for Economic Development in the Horn of Africa*. Trenton, NJ: Red Sea Press.

Waldron, J. (2010) 'Property and Ownership', in Edward N. Zalta (ed.), *The Stanford Encyclopedia of Philosophy*.

Washington, G. (1796) 'The Address of General Washington to The People of The United States on his Declining of the Presidency of the United States', *American Daily Advertiser*.

Weber, M. (1919) *Politik als Beruf (Politics as a Vocation)*. Munich: Duncker & Humblodt.

Whiston, T. (2002) 'Medieval Iceland and the Absence of Government', available at www.mises.org/story/1121.

White, M. (2011a) 'Source List and Detailed Death Tolls for Man-Made Multicides throughout History', available at http://necrometrics.com/warstats.htm.

—. (2011b) 'Death by Mass Unpleasantness: Estimated Totals for the Entire 20th Century', available at http://users.erols.com/mwhite28/warstat8.htm.

Widerquist, K. (2009) 'A Dilemma for Libertarianism', *Politics, Philosophy & Economics,* 8 (1), 43–72.

Wittgenstein, L. (1969) *On Certainty*. G. E. M. Anscombe and G. H. von Wright (eds), Trans. Denis Paul and G. E. M. Anscombe. Oxford: Blackwell.

Zane, D. (2011) 'Somalia: Failed State', available at www.bbc.co.uk/news/world-africa-12278628.

INDEX